A USER-FRIENDLY DICTIONARY OF OLD ENGLISH

THIRD EDITION

COMPILED BY
BILL GRIFFITHS

HEART OF ALBION PRESS

A USER-FRIENDLY DICTIONARY OF OLD ENGLISH

Third edition
Compiled by Bill Griffiths
ISBN 1 872883 25 7
First edition published by author 1989
Third edition published by Heart of Albion Press 1993
Reprinted with minor corrections 1995
Reprinted 1997
© Copyright B. Griffiths 1989, 1993, 1995

Heart of Albion Press
2 Cross Hill Close, Wymeswold
Loughborough, LE12 6UJ

Printed in England by
Newark Chamber of Commerce

SCOPE & AIM

This dictionary contains some three-and-a-half-thousand of the commonest words in Old English (Anglo-Saxon) and should be useful to beginners in translating simple passages of OE prose and verse from any source, as well as to more advanced students as a rapid reference aid.

The *User Friendly Dictionary* lists words by order of the consonants they contain, rather than by the usual strict alphabetical order of all letters in the word. The variation in Old English (OE) in stressed vowels at different times and in different dialects, plus many variants of spellings, make conventional OE dictionaries very tedious to look up words in – you are constantly referred to another entry. This problem is largely eliminated here, and after even a little practice, the user should find this dictionary offers an easy and speedy way to locate OE words.

ORDER OF WORDS

Words are listed by order of their consonants; vowels are only taken into account in ordering words within an identical consonant profile. Inflected endings are generally ignored in establishing the order e.g. the final *-eð* or *-ede* of a verb or *-um* or *-an* of a noun will not be taken into account except in cases like *dōð* where there is little choice. Similarly prefixes e.g. *ā-, on-, be-, ġe-* are usually ignored in listing words, though quite a few common examples will also be found listed under their prefixed forms. Compounds (word-combinations) are not listed as such unless particularly common or with a specialised meaning; otherwise, these should be looked up under their constituent elements which is arguably the best way of understanding how the compound is built anyway.

Summary:

> look for *ġelysteð* and *lāst* under L*S
> look for *wiðcweðan* under W*TH or CW*
> look for *mānscaða* under M*N and SC*, and combine the meanings of the two elements.

1

ABBREVIATIONS

acc.	accusative
adj.	adjective
adv.	adverb
comp.	comparative
conj.	conjunction
dat.	dative case
F.	strong feminine noun
f.	weak feminine noun
gen.	genitive case
I	class 1 weak verbs
II	class 2 weak verbs
indecl.	indeclinable
instr.	instrumental case
M.	strong masculine noun
m.	weak masculine noun
N.	strong neuter noun
n.	weak neuter noun
nom.	nominative
obl.	oblique cases i.e. those other than nominative
p.	preterite or past tense
pl.	plural
pp.	past (or passive) participle
ppl.	preterite (past) plural
pref.	prefix
prep.	preposition
pron.	pronoun
sg.	singular
sim.	similarly
subj.	subjunctive
subst.	substantive (noun)
superl.	superlative

OLD ENGLISH PRONUNCIATION

a (back 'a') short as in German M<u>a</u>nn   long as in f<u>a</u>ther

æ (front 'a') short as in c<u>a</u>t   long as in <u>a</u>dd

e short as in s<u>e</u>t   long as in th<u>ey</u>

i short as in s<u>i</u>t   long as in mach<u>i</u>ne

o short as in f<u>o</u>r   long as in g<u>o</u>

u short as in s<u>oo</u>t   long as in h<u>oo</u>t

y was pronounced like French 'u' ('oo' with rounded lips) or German 'ü'; but in late West Saxon texts, 'y' becomes largely equivalent to 'i' and doubtless was pronounced like 'i'.

Note: unlike Modern English, the short and long forms of each vowel differ only as regards length; the sound of the vowel itself does not alter.

All consonants are sounded: e.g. *cniht* = c+n+i+h+t

The following special combinations should be noted:

sc is pronounced <u>sh</u>   **cc** is pronounced <u>ch</u>   **cg** is pronounced <u>dg</u>

ht is pronounced like <u>kt</u> (better, as in German ni<u>cht</u>)

Note: g and c, in combination with back vowels (a, o, u) are pronounced as in <u>go</u> and <u>k</u>ite. In combination with front vowels (æ, e, i) g and c are pronounced as in <u>y</u>acht and <u>ch</u>eese: these latter (palatalised) forms are marked in the *Dictionary* with a dot, so that

$$\dot{g} = \underline{y} \qquad\qquad \dot{c} = \underline{ch}.$$

Such markings are necessarily tentative; for example, I regard <u>ng</u> as a single sound, not liable to palatalisation, and so give cyni<u>ng</u>e not cyni<u>ṅg</u>e.

Note: there are two forms of the special OE consonant for <u>th</u>: þ ('thorn') and ð ('eth') - in OE usage there are interchangeable.

3

INFLEXIONS

Unlike Modern English, which depends on the order of words in the sentence (sense-order) to convey meaning and fix the grammatical role of each word, OE had built-in word-endings or inflexions that served as markers for the role the word played in the sentence. Sense-order was thus less important in OE (especially in poetry), and eventually the student will have to come to grips with the four cases OE nouns exhibit:

nominative is used for the subject (the actor or doer) of a verb e.g. <u>he</u> ate cheese, the <u>king</u> liked cheese.

accusative is used for the direct object (the victim) of a verb e.g. he ate <u>cheese</u>.

the genitive is the possessive case: the <u>king's</u> cheese, the cheese <u>of Essex.</u>

the dative is used for the indirect object e.g. he gave cheese <u>to the mouse</u>; and for the ablative or causative case e.g. the cheese was eaten <u>by the mouse.</u>

A case-ending in OE therefore often takes the place of words like 'of', 'to', 'by' etc. in Modern English.

Nouns in OE have gender (masculine, feminine, neuter) as in modern German. The principal case endings for 'strong' (mean idiosyncratic or awkward!) nouns are as follows:

Strong Masculine Nouns (singular):
nom. – (no special ending)
acc. – (no special ending)
gen. -es
dat. -e

Strong Masculine Nouns (plural):
nom. – as
acc. -as
gen. -a
dat. -um

Neuter Nouns vary from the Masculine in having *nom./acc.pl.* without ending (compare Modern English plural 'sheep') or in -u, rather than in -as.

Strong Feminine Nouns (singular):
nom. -u (or no ending)
acc. -e
gen. -re
dat. -re

Strong Feminine Nouns (plural)
nom. -a or -e
acc. -a or -e
gen. -ra
dat. -um

4

There is also a group of 'weak' nouns, which have all cases (other than *nom.sg.* and *dat.pl.*) in -an (cf. Modern English plural ox<u>en</u>).

Verbs take endings rather like those preserved in the Authorised King James Bible:

Present Tense: *iċ bind-e* (I bind), *ðū bindest* (you bind), *hē bindeð* (he binds); the plural has just one ending: *bind-að* (we, you, they bind). The 3rd person sg. is often abbreviated in West Saxon to -t e.g. *hē bin-t* besides Anglian *bind-eð*.

Past Tense: as in Modern English, there are two ways of making the past tense. With strong verbs the root vowel alters: *hē bīteð* (he bites) with *hē bit* (he bit); *hē swimmeð* (he swims) with *hē swom* (he swam); with 'weak' verbs a suffix *-ede* (class I) or *-ode* (class II) is added e.g. *hē rīcsað* (he rules) with *hē rīcsode* (he ruled), *hē lufað* (he loves) with *hē lufode* (he loved). A variant is: *hē ðenċeð* (he thinks) with *hē ðōhte* (he thought). The past plural is always *-on* e.g. *lufodon,* etc.

The past participle is formed in *-en* for strong verbs, in *-ed* for weak verbs (much as in Modern English) e.g. *grōwen* (grown), *drifen* (driven), *ascod* (asked). The unstressed prefix *ġe-* is usually added to the past participle e.g. *ġedrifen, ġeascod.*

The principal common suffixes or word-endings are as follows. Note, many of these were already ambiguous in OE, which probably contributed to their decline in use in the change-over into Modern English (M.E.):

A	*gen.pl.* of all nouns, *nom.sg.* of weak nouns
A	*nom. acc.* pl. of Feminine nouns; obl. sg. of some nouns
ADE	ending for past of weak verbs (class II)
AN	infinitive of verb ('to do' etc.)
AN	ending of most cases in weak nouns and adjs.
AS	*nom. acc.* pl. ending of strong masculine nouns (compare M.E. plural in <u>-s</u>)
AÐ	third person sg. ending of present tense of weak verbs (class II)

5

E	*dat.* sg. of strong masculine and neuter nouns.
E	*nom. acc.* pl. of strong feminine nouns, and of all adjectives
E	verb ending in present and past tense
EÐE	ending for past tense of weak verbs (class I)
ES	*gen.* of strong masculine and neuter nouns (compare M.E. 's)
EÐ	third person sg. ending of present tense of verbs (compare biblical 'passeth' etc.)
IAÐ	plural ending of present tense of weak verbs (class II)
OÐE	ending for past tense of weak verbs
ON	plural ending of past tense of verbs
U	*nom. acc.* pl. of strong neuter noun; *nom.* sg. of some strong feminine nouns
UM	*dat.* pl. of all nouns
UM	*dat.* sg. of strong adj.

Here are some of the common demonstrative sē (the, that, those), also used as pronouns (he, she, it, they) and relative (who, what, which).

Singular:

Masc. nom. sg.: Sē	Fem. nom. sg.: Sēo	Neut. nom. sg.: þæt
Masc. acc. sg.: ðone	Fem. acc. sg.: ðā	Neut. acc. sg.: þæt
Masc. gen. sg.: þæs	Fem. gen. sg.: ðǣre	Neut. gen. sg.: þæs
Masc. dat. sg.: þǣm	Fem. dat. sg.: ðǣre	Neut. dat. sg.: þæm

Plural (all genders):

nom.: ðā
acc.: ðā
gen.: ðāra
dat.: þǣm

6

ā/ō   adv. 'ever, always'
ā-   (?a-) unaccented verb
         prefix
ǣ   F. 'law, religion'
ǣ-   'water-; religion-'
ēa   'river' obl. īe
ī-   = ġe-

**B

ebba   m. 'ebb-tide'
abbod   M. 'abbot'
abbodisse f. 'abbess'
ebrisc   adj. 'Hebrew'

**C

āc   M. 'oak (tree)'
ac   conj. 'but; and'
ēċe   adj. 'eternal'
ēac   adv. 'also'
ēaca   m. 'increase'
iċ   pron. 'I'
īeċ-eð   'increases, augments'
           p. ȳcte
ecg   F. 'edge, point; sword';
           as pref. 'sword-'
ācol   adj. 'dismayed, scared'
ēcum/ēcan obl. of ēċe 'eternal'
ācen-ð   I 'gives birth to'
ēacn-að   II 'increases, is enlarged'
ācennednes F. 'birth'
ēacnung   F. 'increase'
ēċnes   F. 'eternity'
æcer   M. 'field, acre' pl. acras
ȳcte   p. 'increased'

**D

ād   'funeral pyre'
ed-   'again'
ēode   p. 'went' pl. ēodon
ēad   N. 'riches, good fortune'
ēad-   = ēad- 'rich' or ēað- 'easy',
         'humble'

ēadiġ   adj. 'blessed, prosperous,
           lucky'
ādl   FN 'disease'
īd(e)l   adj. 'worthless, vain, empty'
edlēan   N. 'reward, recompense'
adūne   adv. 'below; down'
ēaden   pp. 'granted, decreed'
oden   F. 'threshing-floor'
edniwe   adj. 'new, renewed'
ǣdre   adv. 'speedily; entirely'
ēdre/ǣdre f. 'artery'
ādrinċ-eð 'drowns, perishes'
ides   F. 'lady'
edsceaft   F. 'new being, renewal'
edwist   F. 'food, substance'
edwīt   N. 'reproach, abuse'

**F

of   prep.+dat. 'from, out of':
           adv. 'away, off'
of–   'off-, out-'
           (intens./destructive)
of-bēat-an   'to beat to death'
of-ēode   p. 'he obtained, extorted'
of-dæle   N. 'slope, chasm'
of-dōn   'to remove'
of-dūne   adv. 'down'
of-ġief-eð   'gives up, quits'
of-gān   'to obtain, extort'
of-hende   adj. 'absent'
yfel   adj. 'evil'; gen. yfles
yfle   adv. 'evilly, wrongly'
of-feall-an 'to fall on, kill; to fall
           away'
of-leġd   pp. 'laid down'
of-lēt   p. 'gave up'
ofman   p. 'forgot'
yfemest   adj. 'upmost'
ǣfen   M. 'evening' gen. ǣfnes
æfn-a   'performs, achieves'
           p. æfnade
efen   adj/adv 'even, equal'
efn-   'just-as, equally'

efne   adv. 'even, quite, likewise'
ofen   M. 'furnace, oven'
            gen. ofnes
ufan   adv. 'from above, over'
æfnung   F. 'evening'
efenlîca   m. 'equal, like'
efenlæċeð   I 'imitates'
ufanweardum   adv. 'above'
āfȳr   'drive away!'
āfēar-ed   *pp.* 'frightened'
æfre   adv. 'ever, always'
eofor   M. '(wild) boar, boar-helmet'
eafora   m. 'son, heir'
ōfer   M. 'edge, bank, shore'
            gen. ōfres
ofer   prep. 'beyond, over, across';
            adv. 'over, across; in excess'
ofer–   'across, over; very, too
            much'
offr-að   'offers, sacrifices';
            p. offrade
ufor   adv. 'higher'
ofer-brǣd-an   'to spread over,
                overshadow'
ofer-hȳrnes F. 'transgression,
            omission'
ofer-hyġd   FN 'pride, arrogance'
ofer-mōd   adj. 'proud'; subst. 'pride,
            overconfidence'
ofer-mǣte   adj. 'excessive'
ofer-mētto F.*pl.* 'pride'
offrung   F. 'offering'
ofer-sēon   'to survey; look down on;
            reject'
ofer-swîðan I 'to overpower'
ofer-wrēon 'to cover, conceal'
            pp. oferwriġen
of-scēot-eð 'shoots down'
of-slēaᵹ   'to cut off, strike down,
            destroy' *p.* ofslōg,
            pp. ofsleġen
of-snîð-an 'to cut off, kill'
ǣ-fæst   adj. 'pious'

efst   'hastens'
ofost   F. 'haste'
ǣfæstnes   F. 'religion'
oft   adv. 'often'; *sup.* oftost
ofett   N. 'fruit, vegetable'
oftēah   *p.* 'withheld'
æfter   prep.+dat. 'after, according
            to, through'
æfterra   adj. 'following, next'
of-ðynċeð   'it displeases, vexes
            someone'
ufeweard   adj. 'upward'

*G
æġ   N. *pl.* ǣgru 'egg'
æġ-   pref. 'any-'
îġ   F. 'island'
-iġ   adjectival suffix
eġe   M. 'awe, dread, fear'
ēage   n. 'eye'
æġhwelċ   pron. 'each'
æġhwǣr   adv. 'anywhere'
āgōl   *p.* 'yelled out'
āglæca   m. 'monster, demon'
îġlond   M. 'island'
āgan   'to own'
ā-gān   *pp.* 'gone' (gān)
āgen   adj. 'one's own' *gen.* āgnes
ēgor   M. 'flood, ocean'
eġesa   m. 'monster, horror, fear'
eġesliċ   adj. 'frightful'
āgoten   *pp.* 'overlaid'
ā-gǣð   'occurs' (gān)
ǣġþer   pron. 'either, both'
iugoð   F. 'age; youth'
ēage-ðyrel N. 'window'

*H
āh   'owns' (āgan)
ēoh   M. 'yew-tree'
eoh   MN 'war-horse' *gen.* ēos
ā-hebban   'to raise, lift up'
ā-hæfen   *pp.* 'raised' (hebban)

āhte	*p.* 'owned'
ǣht	F. 'possession(s)'
ēht	F. 'hostility, persecution'
ēht-eð	I 'pursues, vexes'
eaht	F. 'esteem, opinion'
eahta	'eight'
eaht-an	'to esteem, consider'; 'to pursue'; *p.* eahtode
īhte	*p.* 'increased'
ūht(e)	Mf. 'half-light, pre-dawn'
ūht-sang	M. 'Matins'
ā-hwǣr	adv. 'anywhere'

*L

al-	= eal 'all'
ele	MN 'oil'
eall	adj. 'all'
eal-	'very-, entirely-'
ēalā	'oh!, alas!'
ealu	N. 'ale' *obl.* ealoð
ele-bēam	M. 'olive-tree'
ǣlċ	adj./pron. 'each'
ōlecc-eð	'flatters'
ōleccung	F. 'flattery, something agreeable'
ālecg-an	I 'to lay down; abolish'
elc-að	'tarries'
elcung	F. 'delay'
elcor	adv. 'elsewhere'
(for)ald-eð	'grows old'
eald	adj. 'old, ancient'
eald-	'former, original, ancient'
ylde	M.*pl.* 'men'
yldo	F. 'age, period; old age'
yldan	'to delay'
yldra	adj. 'older, elder'
yldran	*pl.* 'ancestors'
ealdor	N. 'life'
ealdor	M. 'elder, master' *gen.* ealdres
ealdordom	M. 'lordship'
ealdor-mann	M. 'earl, shire-officer'
yldest	adj. 'oldest'

olfend(a)	Mm 'camel'; or = ylpend 'elephant'
ylfete	F. 'swan'
ealg-að	'defends'
ealh	'temple' *gen.* ēales
eolh	M. 'elk'
eolhsecg	M. 'papyrus, reed'
ǣlmihtiġ	adj. 'almighty'
ǣlmessan	*pl.* 'almsgiving, charity'
ellen	N. 'zeal, valour'
ellen-	'powerful-, heroic-'
elne	adv. 'zealously, keenly'
elniend	adj. 'zesty, increasing in strength'
ellende	adj. 'foreign'
ealneġ	adv. 'always'
ēalond	N. 'island'
eallunga	adv. 'entirely'
ylp/elpend	M. 'elephant'
ellor	adv. 'elsewhere'; adj. 'other'
ealles	adv. 'entirely'
elles	adv. 'otherwise, besides'
eles	*gen.* of ele 'oil'
ālīes-an	I 'to release'
eallswā	adv. '(just) as; also; similarly'
ealoð	*obl.* of ealu 'ale'
elðēode	*pl.* 'foreigners'
elðēodiġ	adj. 'foreign'
ǣlwiht	M. 'monster'

*M

ēam	'(maternal) uncle'
eom	'I am'
ymb(e)	prep/adv. 'about, around; after'
ymb-ċierran	'to revolve'
ymb-gang	M. 'circuit'
ymb-hȳdiġ	adj. 'anxious'
ymb-hoga	m. 'a care, worry'
ymb-hwyrft	M. 'orbit, revolution'
umbor	N. 'infant'
ymb-sittan	'to surround, besiege'

ymb-ūtan	prep/adv. 'around, about'
ōmiġ	adj. 'rusty'
imp-ian	'to graft'
ǣmette	f. 'ant'
ǣmetta	m. 'leisure'

*N

ān	adj./pron. 'one, a'
ann/onn	'grants' *pl.* unnon
ǣnne	*acc.* of ān ('one')
ın	prep. 'in, into, on' etc
ın	adv. 'on, in'
ınn	N. 'lodging'
inne	adv. 'inside'
on	= in
on-	'in-, into–, on-' (but often redundant); 'un-'
ono	'lo!'
unbindan	'to untie'
onbryrd	*pp.* 'excited; incited'
onbūtan	prep./adv. '(a)round, about'
inċ	*acc. dat.* 'you two'
unc	*acc. dat.* 'us two'
incofa	m. 'inner room; heart'
unclǣne	adj. 'unclean, impure'
oncnāweð	'knows, perceives'
	p. oncnēow
āncora	m. 'hermit'
ancor	M. 'anchor'
inċer	'belonging to both of you'
uncer	'belonging to us both'
unċyst	F. 'vice, fault'
uncūð	adj. 'unknown, strange'
oncweðeð/oncwyð	'answers; echoes'
and	conj. 'and'
ānæd	'desert, wasteland'
ende	M. 'end'
ġe-end-að	II 'ends'
endebyrd(nes)	F. 'order, orderliness; development'
ende-dæġ	'day of death'
ondġiet/andġyt	N. 'understanding, meaning'

ondleofen	F. 'food'
endlyfta	'eleventh'
andlēan	N. 'requital'
endemes	adv. 'entirely; together'
ondōn/undōn, ondēð	'to undo; cancel'
under	prep. 'under, beneath, below'
under-fōn	'to accept, undertake'
under-ġieteð	'perceives'
undern	M. 'morning'
undyrne	adj. 'unsecret, public'
understondeð	'understands'
ondrǣt	'fears' (ondrǣdan)
andettan	I 'to acknowledge, confess'
andswar-ian	II 'to answer, reply'
	p. andswarede
andswaru	F. 'an answer'
andwlita	m. 'face, countenance'
andweard	adj. 'present, current'
andwyrdan	I 'to answer'
ānfloga	m. 'solitary flier'
onfōn, onfēhð	'to take, accept'
	p. onfēng
onufon	prep.+*dat.* 'above, upon'
unforcūð	adj. 'honourable'
unfrið	M. 'breach of the peace'
ǣniġ	adj./pron. 'any'
enge	adj. 'narrow, restricted, painful'
uniġ–	= unġe–
inġehyġd	F. 'conscience, thoughts'
engel	M. 'angel' *pl.* englas
unġeliċ	adj. 'unalike'
Engle	M.*pl.* 'Anglians, English'
Angelcyn	N. 'the English'
Englalond	'England'
englisc	adj. 'english, anglo-saxon'
onġyldan	'to pay, make up for'
onġemong	prep.+*dat.* 'among, during'
unġemete	adj./adv. 'immense(ly)'
onġēan	prep./adv. 'opposite, over-, against'

anġinn N. 'beginning'
onġinneð 'begins, sets about' p.ongann
ingang M. 'entry, access'
onġēanweard 'back to'
onġyred pp. 'unfastened'
unġerād adj. 'ignorant, wrong'
onġit-eð 'understands, realises'
   p. onġeat, onġēaton
unġewiss adj. 'inexperienced'
unhold adj. 'disloyal'
unhîere adj. 'horrible, wild'
ānliċ adj. 'special, beautiful'
anlȳċnes F. 'similar thing; statue'
onǣled pp. 'enkindled'
onlāh p. 'loaned'
ānlîpe adj. 'single, individual'
unlȳtel adj. 'quite large'
onlūtan 'to bow, bend'
onmiddan prep.+dat. 'amidst'
ān-mōd adj. 'resolute, single-minded'
onemn prep.+dat. 'alongside, near'
innan prep./adv. 'within, from
   within'
oninnan +dat. 'inside'
ġeunnen pp. 'granted'
ānunga adv. 'straight away; entirely'
onuppan prep.+dat. 'upon'; adv.
   'additionally'
ānrǣd adj. 'resolute'
unrǣd M. 'folly'
unriht adj./subst. 'wrong'
unriht-hǣmed N. 'adultery'
unrîm N. 'a countless number'
onrǣs M. 'onrush'
unrōt adj. 'sad'
onsæ̇ġednes F. 'sacrifice, offering'
ansîen F. 'visage, face, appearance'
ansund adj. 'sound, healthy'
onsendan I 'to send, forward'
onspon p.'unfastened, revealed'
onsæt p. 'occupied; menaced'
onsteal M. 'a supply'
onstell-an I 'to ambush'

instæpes adv. 'directly'
onstyred pp. 'agitated'
ent M. 'giant'
onett-eð I 'hastens'
unnyt adj. 'useless'
antimber 'material, substance'
ontȳned pp. 'opened'
intinga m. 'subject, reason'
untrum adj. 'infirm, ill'
untwēoġendliċ adj. 'certain'
innoð MF 'insides, womb'
unēaðe adj. 'difficult, hard'
unǣðele adj. 'ignoble, common'
unþonc M. 'ingratitude, disservice'
unþēaw M. 'vice, sin'
onweġ adv. 'away'
onweald/anwald M. 'authority, power'
unwillum adv. 'reluctantly'
unwealt adj. 'unstable'
inweard adj. 'inner'
unwearnum adv. 'unstoppably'
unweorð adj. 'worthless'
inwit N. 'malice, wickedness'

*P
ūp/upp adv. 'up'
uppe adv. 'above'
ypp-eð 'opens, discloses, reveals'
   pp. ypped
ūp-āhebban 'to lift or raise up'
æppl M. 'apple' pl. applas
ūplond N. 'country, rural area'
open adj. 'open, evident, clear'
uppon adv. 'from above/upon'
openliċ adj. 'plain, public'
apostol M. 'apostle'
epistola m. 'letter'
ūpweard(es) adv. 'upwards'

*R

ār	M. 'messenger'; 'honour, mercy'; 'oar'; N. 'copper'
ār-að	II 'honours, spares'
ǣr	adv./prep. 'before, already'
ēar	'ocean'/'earth'
ēare	n. 'ear'
er-að	'plows' *p.* erede
or–	'without; ancient'
ōr	N. 'beginning, start'
ōra	m. 'border, edge'; 'ore'
ūr	M. 'aurochs, bison'
ūre	adj. 'our'
yrre	'anger, wrath' *gen.* yrres; adj. 'angry'
ark/earc	Ff 'chest; ark'
orc	M. 'ghoul'; 'cup'
ærċebiscop	M. 'archbishop'
eorcnan-stān	M. 'precious stone'
orcnǣwe	adj. 'well-known'
orċeard	M. 'orchard'
ārod	adj. 'honoured'
arod	adj. 'prompt, quick'
eard	M. 'native land, home, place'
eard-að	'inhabits'; *p.* eardode
-eardiend	'-dweller'
eardung	F. 'abode'
ēored	NF 'mounted troop'
ord	M. 'point (e.g. of origin); front-rank; source'
ordfruma	m. 'start, origin'
orf	N. 'cattle' etc.
yrfe	N. 'inheritance, heritage'
aræfnan	'to perform'
earfoðe	N. 'hardship, trouble'; adj. 'difficult, hard'
earfoð-	'difficult-to, hard-to'
eriġean	'to plow' *p.* erede
earg/earh	adj. 'cowardly, rotten'
earh	F. 'arrow'
eorl	M. '(brave) man; earl'
eorl-liċ	adj. 'manly'
orleġe	adj. 'hostile'; N. 'contention'

ārlēas	adj. 'impious'
earm	M. 'arm'
earm	adj. 'wretched, vile'
ormōd	adj. 'hopeless, in despair'
yrmde	*p.* 'harassed'
eormen-	'powerful-, huge-'
yrming	M. 'wretch'
ormǣte	adj. 'huge, immoderate'
yrmð(u)	F. 'misery'
arn	*p.* 'ran'
ærn	N. 'hall; room'
earon	'are'
earn	M. 'eagle'
īren	N. 'iron'
iernan, irn-ð	'runs' *p.* arn, urnon
ǣrende	M. 'message, errand'
yringa	adv. 'in anger'
ġeearnung	'merit, desert'
ǣrist	'resurrection'
eornoste	adj. 'earnest, serious'
orped	adj. 'decisive, active'
orsorg	adj. 'unconcerned, carefree'
ǣrest	adj. 'first, earliest'
eart	'are'
ōret	M. 'fight'
ōřetta	m. 'warrior'
ortrȳwe	adj. 'hopeless; faithless'
eorðe	f. 'earth, soil, world'
eorð-	'of this world'
oroð	N. 'breath(ing)'
yrð	F. 'plowing; crop'
eorðliċ	adj. 'earthly'
yrðling	M. 'ploughman'
orðang	N. 'intelligence, cleverness'
orðung	F. 'breath'
ǣr-ðan-ðe	conj. 'before'
orwēna	adj.+*gen.* 'in despair (of)'

*S

assa	m. 'ass'
ǣs	N. 'food'
īs	N. 'ice'
is/ys	'is'

ūs	acc. dat. 'us'
æsc	'ash (tree); object made of ash, boat, spear'
āskian/āscian	'to ask' p. āscode
ġe-ascian	II 'to hear of, learn of'
yslan	pl. 'embers'
esne	M. 'common man, servant'
īsen	N. 'iron'
ūsser	'our'
īsern	N. 'iron'
ēst	F. 'favour, approval'
ēast	adv. 'east (wards)'
ȳst	F. 'storm, tempest'
astīhð	'climbs' p. astāh; (stîgan)
ēastan	adv. 'easterly, from the east'
ostre	f. 'oyster'
Eastron	f.pl. 'Easter'
Eastseaxe	pl. 'East Saxons, Essex'
ēast(e)weard	'eastwards'

*T

ǣt	'food'
æt	prep. 'at, by, from'
it-eð, itt, eteð	'eats (up)'
ūt	adv. 'out'
ūtāberstan	'to break out'; sim. ætberstan
ūtādōn	'to put out'
ūtdrîfeð	'drives away'
ætforan	prep. 'in front of, before'
ætgædere	adv. 'together'
ætġifa	m. 'food provider'
ūtgang	M. 'exit'
atol	adj. 'awful, fearful'
ȳtemest	adj. 'ultimate, uttermost'
eoten	M. 'giant'
ūtan	adv. '(from) outside'
ūtanweard	'outside'
ātor	N. 'poison' gen. āttres
ūter(r)a	adj. 'outer'
ǣtren	adj. 'poisonous'
ætîewde/ætēowde	p. 'displayed'
ūteweard	adj. 'external'

*TH

āð	pl. -as 'oath'
ēaðe/ēðe	adj. 'easy'; adv. 'easily'
ēð-/ēað-	'easy-to'
ēð-an	'to breathe' p. ēðedon
îeð	adv. 'more easily'
oð	prep. 'up to, as far as, until'; conj. 'until'
oð-	'apart-, away-'
oððe	conj. 'or'
ūðe	pl. ūðon 'granted'
ȳð	F. 'wave; water'
ȳð-beġeata	adj. 'easily obtained'
oðbeoreð	'bears away'
oðfealleð	'fails; declines'

[*TH]

æðele	adj. 'noble'
ēðel	MN 'own land or home' gen. ēðles
ēaðeliċ	adj. 'simple, unimportant'
æðeling	M. 'princeling, noble'
ēaðmettu	F. 'humility'
ēaðmōd	adj. 'gentle, kind'
āðenian	'to stretch, draw out'
ōðer	adj./pron. 'other, another, the second; some ... some' gen. ōðres
āuðer	pron. 'someone, anyone/thing'; conj. 'either... or...'
oððæt	conj. 'until'
oðîew-an	'to demonstrate; appear' p. oðîewde
ūðwita	m. 'scholar, philosopher'

*W

āwa	adv. 'for ever'
ēow	acc./dat. 'you, to you'
āwecc-an	'to awake, make rise' p. awehte
ēowde/ēwed	FN 'flock of sheep'
ġeȳwed	pp. 'shown'
aweġ	adv. 'away'

āwiht	adv. 'at all'; subst. 'anything'
āwerġed	pp. 'accursed'
ēower	adj. 'your'

*X

ax-ian	'to ask' p. axode
æx/æcs	F. 'axe' pl. axe
eax/ex	F. 'axle, axis'
oxa	m. 'ox'
eaxl	F. 'shoulder'
axan	pl. 'ashes'

B*

bā	adj. 'both'
be/bī	+dat. 'by, about, along'
be-	pref. makes vb. trans. etc.
bēo	'be!'
bēo	f. 'bee'

B*B

bebod	N. 'command'

B*C

bæċ	N.'back'; pl. bacu; under bæċ 'behind'
bēċe	F. 'beech'
bōc	F. 'book' pl. bēċ
bucca	m. 'goat'
bæċbord	N. 'port (side)'
bycgan	I 'to buy'
bōcland	N. 'land by title, alienable land'
becum-að	'arrives, meets, happens' p. becōm
bēacn	N. 'sign, banner, symbol'
bīecn-að	'signals, signifies'
bæċere	M. 'baker'
bōcere	M. 'scholar'
bōc-cræft	M. 'learning'

B*D

bād	p. 'awaited' (bīdan)
bæd-eð	'urges, requires'

bæd, bǣdon	p. 'asked' (bidan)
ġebed	N. 'prayer' pl. ġebedu
bedd	N. 'couch'
ġebedda	m. 'bedfellow, mate'
bēad	p. 'offered' (bēodan)
beadu	F. 'war, battle' gen. beadwa/beaduwe
bēod	M. 'bowl, table'
bēod-eð/bīett	'offers, declares, orders' +dat.; p. bēad
bīd-eð	'waits' p. bād pp. ġebiden
gebīd-eð	'experiences'
bid-eð	'asks' p. bæd, bǣdon
gebid-eð	'prays' p. ġebidde
ġebod	N. 'command'
boda	m. 'messenger'
bod-að	II 'preaches, declares' p. bodade
būde, būdon	'dwelt'; 'bent'
bydel	M. 'messenger'
bodung	F. 'preaching'

B*F

bifian	II 'trembled, shuddered' p. bifode
bufan	prep. 'above'
beforan	+dat. 'before, ahead of'
beæftan	+dat. 'behind'

B*G

bēag/bēg	M. 'ring, arm-ring'
bēag	p. 'bent' (būgan)
bēġ-ð	= būg-eð 'bends'
begãð	'does, serves' etc (begãn)
biġ	= be 'by' etc
bīeġ-eð	'turns; makes bend' p. bīġde/bēġde
bȳġ-eð	'dwells'
būg-eð	'bends, bows' p. bēag
bēġde	p. 'turned' (bīegan)
begãn	'to cross; inhabit, attend to, cultivate; pratice, worship'

bēġen   adj. 'both'
beginn-eð   'to begin' p. began
beġeondan   prep. 'beyond'
bīgeng   F. 'observance, habit'
bigong   M. 'circuit, region'
bōg   M. 'bough'; 'arm'
boga   m. 'bow'
bēgra   'of both'
beġieteð   'obtains; begets'

B*H

bēah   = bēag ('ring')
bōh   = bōg 'bough; arm'
behōfað   'it behoves, is necessary'
behēafdod   pp. 'beheaded'
behealdeð   'gazes on, preserves'
beheonan   +dat. 'on this side of'
bōhte   p. 'bought'
behāteð   'promises'

B*L

bǣl   N. 'fire, bonfire'
belle   m. 'bell'
bealu   F. 'harm, injury, evil';
   pl. bealwa; adj. 'harmful,
   evil'
bealo-   'wicked, harmful'
bill   M. 'sword, chopper'
bolla   m. 'bowl'
bealċeð   'belches (out)'
bælċ   M. 'pride'
belūc-eð   'shuts up, locks in'
bulluc   M. 'bullock'
bold   N. 'house, hall'
beald/bald   adj. 'bold'
bield-eð   'exhorts; builds'
ġebyld   pp. 'emboldened'
byldo/bieldu   F. 'boldness, arrogance'
baldlīċe   adv. 'boldly'
baldor   M. 'lord'
bīleofa   m. 'support, food'
beliġ-eð   'surrounds' (belicgan)
ġebelg   M. 'anger'

ġebolgen   pp. 'swolen with emotion;
   angered, enraged'
belhð   'angers' (belgan)
belimp-eð   'belongs; happens'
bolster   MN 'cushion, pillow'
   gen. bolstres
belīð   'surrounds' (belicgan)
bilewit   adj. 'pure-minded'
bealwa   pl. of bealu 'harm'
balzam   'balsam'

BL*

blēo   N. 'hue, colour, show'
   gen. blēos dat.pl. blēowum
blāc   adj. 'pale, shiny'
blæċ   adj. 'black'
blīċ-eð   'shines'
blæċ-ern   N. 'lantern'
blǣd   M. 'success, fame'; 'breath,
   blast'
blēd   F. 'fruit, crop'
bledu   F. 'bowl'
blōd   M. 'blood'
blōma   m. 'nugget'
blend-eð   'blinds'
blinn-eð   'ceases, tails off'
blind   adj. 'blind'
ġeblond   N. 'swirl'
ġeblonden   pp. 'mixed, blended'
blonden-feax   adj. 'grizzle-haired'
bliss   F. 'joy'
blissode   +gen. 'rejoiced (in)'
   ('blissian')
blǣst   M. 'blast (of wind, fire)'
blōstma   m. 'flower'
blāt   adj. 'ghastly, livid'
blōt   N. 'sacrfice'
blēts-ian   'to bless' p. blētsode
blētsung   F. 'blessing'
blīþe   adj. 'happy'; sim. blīþful
blāw-eð   'blows' p. blēow
blōw-eð   'blooms' p.blēow pp blōwen

B*M

bâm/bæm	*dat.* 'to both'
bēam	M. 'tree, beam'
bēom	'I am'
bīeme	f. 'trumpet'

B*N

bān	N. 'bone'
bana	m. 'killer'
bann-an	'to summon'
ġebann	N. 'summons, ordinance'
bēn	F. 'petition'
benn	F. 'wound'
bēan	F. 'bean, pea'
bēon	'to be'
binn	F. 'container, manger'
būan	'to dwell'
būne	f. 'beaker'
benċ	F. 'bench'
bān-cofa	m. 'body'
bend	'bond, chain'
bindeð/bint	'binds' *p.* band
	pp. ġebunden
bōnda	m. 'freeman, commoner'
-būende	'-dwellers'
bān-hring	M. 'vertebra'
benām	*p.+gen./dat.* 'deprived'
	(beniman)
bint	'binds' (bindan)
binnan	+*dat.* 'within, inside'
beneoðan	+*dat.* 'beneath'

B*R

bār	M. 'boar'
bar-um	etc. *obl.* of bær 'bare'
gebǣre	N. 'bearing, behaviour; outcry'
-bǣre	(suff.) '-carrying'
bær	adj. 'bare' *obl.* bar–
ber-að	'bares' *p.* berode
ber-eð	'bears' *pp.* ġeboren
bera	m. 'bear'
bere	M. 'barley'

bearu	M. 'grove of trees'
	gen. bearwes
bēor	N. 'beer'
ġebēoras	M*pl.* 'drinking companions'
–bora	'doer'
būr	N. 'room, chamber'
ġebūr	M. 'peasant-farmer'
gebyrað	'belongs, suits, happens' (ġebyrian)
beorc	F. 'birch-tree'
berād	*p.* 'overtook (on horseback)'
beard	M. 'beard'
bord	N. 'shield'; 'plank, deck'
borda	m. 'edge'
ġebyrd	F. 'birth, status'
beriġ	N. 'berry'
bearg	M. 'hog'
beorg	M. 'hill'
ġebeorg	N. 'protection, defence'
beorg-eð	'protects, saves'
	pp. ġeborgen
burg	'borough, walled town'
	dat. byrig
ġebirġeð	'tastes'
ġebyrġed	*pp.* 'buried'
bebyrġan	I 'to bury'
byrgen	F. 'burial, grave'
burgware	*pl.* 'citizens'
bearh	*p.* 'protected'
burh	= burg 'fortress etc.'
bierht-eð	'brightens, illuminates'
birhtu	F. 'brightness'
beorht	adj. 'bright, clear, fine'
bearhtm	M. 'flash (of light, sound)'
byrele	m. 'butler'
bearm	M. 'bosom'
beorma	m. 'yeast'
bierneð	'burned' *p.* barn
bearn	N. 'child'
beorn	M. 'man, soldier'
birn-eð	'burns'
ġeboren	*pp.* 'born'
burne	f. 'stream'

byren	F. 'she-bear'
byrne	f. 'chest-armour, mail-shirt'
berȳp-eð	'takes, strips' p. berȳpte
ġebēorscipe	M. 'company of drinkers'
bersteð	'bursts, crashes' p. bærst
byrst	'great loss or damage'

BR*

brū	= brēaw 'brow'
bræċ	N. 'a breaking'
gebræċ	N. 'clash, noise'
breċ-eð/briċð	'breaks'
	p. bræċ, bræcon
brōc	M. 'brook'
broc	N. 'affliction, adversity, illness'
broc	'badger'
bruċ-eð	'uses, enjoys' +gen. p. brēac
brȳċe	N. 'advantage, profit'; adj. 'useful'
bryce	M 'infringement'
brycg	F. 'bridge'
brac-hwîl	'short time'
ġebrocen	pp. 'broken'
brād	adj. 'wide, broad'
bræd	'flesh'
bræd-eð	'spreads' p. brædde
brēd-eð	'draws, flexes, weaves' p. brūdon pp. brōden
bred	F. 'plank; tablet'
brid	M. 'chick'
brȳd	F. 'bride'
brîdl	M. 'rein'
brēg-að	'alarms, scares'
brego	M. 'prince, chieftain'
brōga	m. 'terror, danger'
breġdeð	'draws, flexes; breeds' (= brēdeð); ppl. brugdon
briġd	N. 'fluctuation of colour'
brōhte	p. 'brought' (bringan)
breahtm	M. 'loud noise'
brēme	adj. 'famous'
brim	N. 'sea'

brēm(b)el	M. 'bramble'
brimðisa	m. 'ship'
brūn	adj. 'dark-and-glossy'
bryne	M. 'a burning'
brand	M. 'sword, torch, fire'
brengeð/bringeð	I 'brings'
brant	adj. 'deep, steep'
brerd	M. 'rim, margin'
brord	M. 'point, shaft'
bryrd-eð	'incites'
brosn-að	II 'decays, rots'
brosnung	F. 'decay'
brēost	M. 'breast, heart'
brastl-að	II 'crackles'
brēt/brîtt	= brēd-eð 'flexes'
brytta	m. 'distributor, giver'
bryttian	II 'to divide up; to rule'
bryten-	(pref.) 'spacious'
Bryt(en)lond	N. 'Britain'
Bryttas/Brettas	pl. 'Britons, Celts'
brēoteð	'demolishes' pp.-broten
bræð	M. 'scent, vapour'
ābrēoþan	'to decay, deteriorate'
brōþor	M. 'brother' dat. brēþer
gebrōþru	Mpl 'brothers, monks'
brēaw	M. 'eye-brow, -lash'

B*S

basu	adj. 'intense red' obl. basw—
bisceop	M. 'bishop'
bescēawað	II 'scans'
bisgu	F. 'preoccupation'
bysgað	'is busy, troubles someone' pp. bysgad
beseah	p. 'looked' (sēon)
bōsm	M. 'bosom'
bismer	M. 'insult, humiliation'
bismr-að	'insults, degrades'
bȳsen/bîsn	F. 'example, model'
ġebȳsnung	F. 'example'
besenċte	p. 'made sink, drowned'
bîspell	N. 'example, fable'

bist–   'you are, will be'
besiteð   'besieges' *pp.* beseten

B*T

bāt   FM 'boat'
bāt   *p.* 'bit' (bītan)
bæteð   'bridles'; 'worries at'
   p. ġebæt *pp.* ġebæted
ġebēteð   *p.* ġebētte 'atones for,
   compensates'
bet   adv. 'better'
bēateð   'beats' *ppl.* bēoton
bēot   N. 'vow, boast, threat'
bît/bîteð   'bites' *p.* bāt, biton
bit   = bideð 'asks'
bite   M. 'bite, sting, cut'
bōt   F. 'cure, remedy'
būtū   pron. 'both'
betæċeð   'entrusts'
bēotiġan   'to boast, pretend'
betæhte   *p.* 'entrusted'
botl   = bold 'building, hall'
bytleð   I, II 'builds'
betliċ   adj. 'excellent'
bēotliċ   adj. 'arrogant, aggressive'
botm   M. 'bottom, foundation'
būtan   +*dat.* 'except'; conj. 'unless,
   except'
ġebiten   *pp.* 'bitten'
betera   adj. 'better'
bitter   adj. 'harsh'
butere   f. 'butter'
betst   adv./adj. 'best, most'
betwēonum   +*dat.* 'between'
betweox/betwix/betweoh +*dat.*
   'between'; betwix þæm þe
   'while'

B*TH

bæð   N. 'bath' *pl.* baþu
biþ   *pl.* bēoþ 'is, will be; are'
boþen   'rosemary'

B*W

bȳw-eð   'polishes'
bewunden   *pp.* 'surrounded'
bewriġen   *pp.* 'covered'
bîwist   F. 'food'
bewitiġeð   'supervises'

C*

cū   F. 'cow' *pl.* cȳ

C*C

ċēac   'jug'
ċēace   f. 'cheek, jaw'
cuiċ/cwiċ   adj. 'alive' *obl.* cucu
ācuc-iað   'they bring to life'
ċycen   N. 'chicken'
cȳdde   *p.* 'declared, made known'

C*D

ġecîd   N. 'argument'
ċîdde   *p.* 'chided; quarreled'
cudu   'cud'

C*F

cāf   adj. 'active, energetic, bold';
   sim. cāfliċ
cofa   m. 'cupboard, cave'
ċeafl   M. 'jaw/cheek(-bone)'

C*G

cæġ   F. 'key'
ċîġeð   'calls' *p.* ċîġde *pp.* ġeċîeġed

C*H

ċehhetung   F. 'laughter, guffawing'

19

C*L

ċēleð	'cools'
ċēol	M. 'ship'
ceole	F. 'throat'
ċiele	M. 'coolness'
cōl	adj. 'cool'
cōl-ian	II 'to grow cool'
col	N. 'coal'
cyll	F. 'leather bottle'
caliċ	M. 'chalice'
ċealc	M. 'chalk, lime'
ċeald	adj. 'cold'
ċild	N. 'child'
ċealf	'calf'
culfer	pl. culfran 'dove'
cylen	'kiln, oven'
collenferhð	adj. 'proud, exultant'
columnan	pl. 'pillars'

CL*

clēa	= clawu 'claw'
clūd	M. 'mass, lump'
clif	N. 'cliff, rock'
clēofeð	'cleaves, splits' ppl. clufon
tōclīfst	'you split up'
clomm	M. 'fetter, chain, grip'
clymmeð	'climbs'
clǣne	adj. 'pure, clean'
cling-eð	'adheres, shrinks' p. clang pp. clungen
clǣns-að	'cleans, purges'
clip-að	'calls out' p. cleopode
(be)clyppeð	I 'to embrace'
clerichād	M. 'priesthood'
cluster	'bar; cell'
clāð	M. 'cloth; clothes'
clawu	F. 'claw' dat.pl. clawum/clām

C*M

cum-eð/cymð 'comes, arrives'
p. cōm(on)/cwōm(on)
pp. ġecymen

cuma	m. 'new arrival, guest'
cyme	M. 'arrival'
camp	'battle, conflict'
cempa	m. 'soldier, champion'
campstede	M. 'battlefield'
cumbol	N. 'standard, banner'
comēta	'comet'

C*N

can	'knows how to, can' pl. cunnon
ċēn	M. 'torch'
cēne	adj. 'bold, brave'
cen-eð	'gives birth to, creates' p. cenede
cunn-an	'to know how to'
cunn-ian, cunn-að	'tries, tests' pp. ġecunnad
cyne-	'royal-'
cyn	N. 'kind, species, breed; kin, people'
-cund	'-like'
ġecynd	F. 'own nature, type'
ġecynde	adj. 'natural'
candel	M. 'candle, lamp'
cynliċ	adj. 'fitting'
cyneliċ	adj. 'royal'
canonbōc	M. 'church rule book'
cyning	M. 'king'
cynren	N. 'kindred'
Cent	'Kent'
Cantware	pl. 'Kentish folk'
Cantwaraburg	F. Canterbury

CN*

ġecnucod	pp. 'pounded, knocked'
cnōdan	'to attribute to'
cniht	M. 'youth, servant'
cnapa	m. 'youth, servant'
cnearr	M. 'small ship'
cnēoris	F. 'generation; people'
cnysseð	'tosses, crashes' pp. ġecnysed/cnissed

cnōsl	N. 'offspring'
cnotta	m. 'knot'
cnāweð	'knows' p. cnēow
cnēow	F. 'knee'

C*P

cēp-eð	'seizes, guards, keeps, accepts'
ċēap	M. 'cattle; any commodity'
ċīep-eð	'trades, buys, sells'
ġecōpliċ	adj. 'correct, proper'
ċīepeman	M. 'merchant'
cypera	pl.-n '(female) salmon'

C*R

caru	F. 'care, concern'
ċierr	M. 'time, change'
ċier-eð	'turns, alters, converts' p. ċierde
cyre	M. 'choice'
ċiriċe	f. 'church'
carc-ern	N. 'prison'
ċeorf-eð	'carves, cuts down' p. ċearf, curfon pp. corfen
carful	adj. 'anxious, diligent'
cariġ	adj. 'anxious'
ċeorl	M. 'churl, peasant, man, freeman'
ċirm	M. 'outcry'
curon	ppl. 'chosen' pp. ġecoren
corn	N. 'seed, tiny grain'
corðor	F. 'troop' pl. corðre

CR*

crabba	m. 'crab'
cræft	M. 'strength, skill, art'
cræftiġ	adj. 'powerful, cunning, learned'
cræft(i)ga	m. 'workman, craftsman'
crang	pl. crungon 'fell, collapsed' (cringan)
crēopeð	'creeps'
cristalla	m. 'crystal'

crîsten	adj. 'Christian'
cristes mæl	'sign of the cross'
cræt	N. 'waggon'

C*S

ċēse	'cheese'
ċēos-eð	'chooses' p. ċēas, curon pp. ġecoren
cyss-eð	I 'kisses'
ċeosel	'gravel, sand'
cosp	M. 'fetter'
cysp-eð	'fetters'
cāsere	M. 'emperor'
ċist	F. 'chest'
ċīest/ċȳst	'chooses' (ċēosan)
ċyst	F. 'the best, an elite'
ċystiġ	adj. 'virtuous, generous'
cost	M. 'option, contingency'
cost-að	II 'tempts'
castel	M. 'castle, fortified town'
cost(n)ung	F. 'temptation; affliction'
ċeaster	F. 'city' gen. ċeastre
ċeaster-ware or -waran	pl. 'citizens'

C*Ð

ċīð	M. 'shoot, sprout'
coðu	F. 'disease'
cūþ	adj. 'well-known, familiar, evident'
cūþe	'knew (how to)' pl. cūþon
cȳðð	F. 'homefolk, homeland'
cȳð-eð/cȳðð	'declares, tells' p. cȳþde
cȳðere	M. 'martyr'

C*W

ċēow-eð	'chews'

CW*

cwiċ	adj. 'living'
cweċ-eð	'shakes'
cwide	M. 'saying, proverb etc'
cwedol	adj. 'talkative'
cwiċ-seolfor	N. 'mercury'

cwæde   pl. cwǣdon 'said'
         pp. ġecweden (from
         cweðan)
cweht   pp. 'shaken'
cwalu   F. 'violent death'
cwel-eð 'kills' ppl. cwealdon
cwyld   'pestilence, destruction'
cwealm   MN 'death, murder, plague'
cwielm-eð 'tortures, kills'
ġecwēme adj. 'agreeable'
cwēm-eð 'pleases'
cwōm   p. 'came'
ācwan   p. 'dwindled'
cwēn   F. 'wife, woman, queen'
cwene   f. 'woman, servant'
ācwenċan   I 'to extinguish'
cweorn   F. 'quern, handmill'
cweart-ern   N. 'prison'
cwȳsan   I 'to crush, destroy'
cwið/cweðeð   'says, speaks'
cwæð   p. 'said'

D*
dō   'do!' (dōn)

D*C
dīċ   'ditch, dike'
dīacon   M. 'deacon'

D*D
dǣd   F. 'deed, act'
dēad   adj. 'dead'
dyde   'did' etc pl. dydon
dǣdbōt   F. 'penance, atonement'
dēadliċ adj. 'perishable, mortal;
         deadly'

D*F
ġedēfe   adj. 'fitting, suitable'
dēaf   adj. 'deaf'
dēaf   p. 'dived'

dēofol   M. 'devil' gen. dēofles
dēofol-ġield   N. 'idolatory; idol'
ġedafen-að   'befits' +dat.
ġedafenliċ   adj. 'fitting, proper'

D*G
dag-að   'it dawns'
dæġ   M. 'day(time) pl. dagas
dēag   pl. dugon 'is good, useful, is
         worth' p. dohte
ġedīġ-eð 'endures, survives'
dæġhwāmliċ   adj. 'daily'
dīgol   adj. 'secret, hidden'
dīeġlað 'hides, conceals'
dugon   ppl. 'availed'
dēagung F. 'dye'
dōgor   M. 'day'
dæġ-red N. 'daybreak'
dæġ-rîm N. 'a number of days'
duguð   F. 'retinue, nobility; host;
         excellence'

D*H
dēah   = dēag 'is good, useful, serves'
diht   N. 'a dictate; disposition'
ġediht   N. 'something written'
ġediht-eð 'disposes; imposes;
         composes'
dohte   'served, was useful'
dohtor   Γ. 'daughter' dat.sg. dehter

D*L
ġedāl   N. 'sharing-out; a difference'
(tō)dǣl-eð   I 'divides, shares out'
bedǣl-eð 'deprives' +gen.
dǣl   M. 'portion, part, area'
         pl. dǣlas
dæl   N. 'valley' pl. dalu
dol   adj. 'silly'
dolliċ   adj. 'foolish, rash'
delfeð   'digs' p. dealf
dolg/dolh   MN 'wound, scar'
dîl(e)gað   'obliterates' pp. (ā)dȳlegod

D*M

dēm-eð 'judges, decrees' p. dēmde
dēma m. 'judge'
demm M. 'injury, loss'
dimm adj. 'dim, gloomy'
dōm M. 'judgement, decree; glory
–dom gen. –dōmes: abstract suffix

D*N

Dēne Mpl. 'the Danes'
denu F. 'valley'
dōn, hē dēð 'do, put, cause, make'
p. dyde
ġedōn pp. 'done, accomplished'
dūn F. 'hill'
ofdūne adv. 'downwards'
dun(n) adj. 'of a dingy colour'
dynede p. 'boomed'
dincge m. 'dung'
denisc adj. 'Danish, Viking'
dynt M. 'blow [or its effect]'

D*P

dēop adj. 'deep, serious'
deōpliċ adj. 'profound'

D*R

daru F. 'injury, damage' gen. dære
Dēre Mpl. 'the Deirans'
der-eð 'to damage, harm' p. ðerede
dear pl. durron 'dares, presumes'
p. dorste
dēor N. 'wild animal; deer'
dēore adj. 'dear, precious'
dor N.'door, passage'
duru FN 'door' pl. dura/duru
dyrre subj. 'might dare'
deorc adj. 'dark, obscure, sinister'
ġedeorf N. 'difficulty, danger'
dēorling M. 'favourite'
durum dat.pl. of duru 'door'
dēormōd adj. 'courageous, worthy'

durron ppl.'they dare'
dyrne adj. 'secret, problematical, wrong'
dorste p. 'dared'
dyrstiġ adj. 'adventurous'
daroð F. 'javelin, spear'
dēor-wyrðliċ adj. 'precious, splendid'

DR*

drȳ M. 'sorcerer'
draca m. 'dragon, serpent'
dreċ-eð 'troubles'
drȳ-cræft 'magic'
ġedrēfed pp. 'stirred up, agitated'
ġedrēfednes F. 'tribultaion'
drîfeð 'drives (out)' p. drāf
drag-an 'to drag, draw'
ġedræġ N. 'throng'
drēog-eð 'works, lives, experiences'
p. drēag pl. drugon
drȳġe adj. 'dry'
drȳġ-eð 'dries' pp. drūgod
(ā)drîh-ð = drēogeð
dryht F. 'large crowd, people'
dryhtguma m. 'warrior, retainer'
dryhten M. 'ruler, lord, esp. God'
drihtnēum dat.pl. 'corpses'
drihtscipe M. 'bravery'
drohtað M. 'way of life, context'
sim. drohtnung
drēam M. 'joy, ecstasy, music'
drȳman I 'to sing aloud'
drenċ-eð I 'supplies drink; drowns
someone'
drinc M. 'drink'
drinċ-eð 'he drinks' p. dranc
ādrinċ-eð 'perishes by drowning'
ġedruncen pp. 'drunk'
dreng M. 'young warrior'
drep-eð 'strikes down'
drep M. 'a blow, stroke'
drēop-eð 'drips'
dropa m. 'a drop; pl. = dew'

dryre M. 'falling, cessation'
drēoriġ adj. 'miserable; blood-stained'
drēorung F. 'falling'
druron *ppl.* see next word:
drēos-eð 'fails, perishes, gives out'
   p. drēas *pl.* druron
drūsade *p.* 'drowsed'
drȳs *gen.* of drȳ 'sorceror'
drysmaþ II 'glowers'

D*S
disc M. 'dish'
dysiġ adj. 'foolish, stupid'
dysgað 'commits errors'
dēst 'you do, make'
dūst N. 'dust'

D*TH
dēað M. 'death'
dēð 'he does, makes' *p.* dyde

D*W
dēaw 'dew'
dēawiġ adj. 'dewy'

DW*
dwel -eð *p.* dwelede 'leads or goes
   astray; deceives'
   sim. dwelað, dwolað
ġedwol adj. 'heretical'
ġedwola m. 'error, heresy'
dwollic adj. 'silly; heretical'
ġedwild N. 'error, heresy'
dweorg M. 'dwarf'
ġedwæs adj. 'stupid, silly'
dwæsceð 'extinguishes'

F*
fēa 'few'
(ġe)fēa M. 'joy'
fēo 'money' (= fēoh)

F*C
fæċ N. 'an interval of time'
   gen.pl. faca
fecċ-eð 'fetches, gets'
fāc(e)n N. 'deceit, treachery, crime'
   pl. fācnu
fǣcne adj. 'treacherous'

F*D
fad-að II 'supervises, arranges'
fēd-eð/fētt 'feeds' *p.* fēdde *pp.* ġefēd
fēode *p.* 'hated'
fōda m. 'food'
ġefadung F. 'organising'
fæder M. 'father'; eald– 'grandfather'
fōddor N. 'food, fodder'

F*F
fīf 'five'
fīfel N. 'large sea-monster'
fēf(e)r 'fever'
fīftiġ 'fifty'

F*G
fāg adj. 'spotted, speckled'
fāg = fāh 'inimical, stained'
fǣġe adj. 'doomed, fated'
ġefēġ N. 'joint'
fēġ-eð 'joins, unites'
fēog·eð 'hates'
fugol M. 'bird, fowl' *pl.* fuglas
fugoloð 'fowling'
fæġn-að II 'rejoices, is happy' +*gen.*
ġefæġen +*gen.* 'glad (at, of)'
fæġer adj. 'fair, lovely'
fæġre adv. 'prettily, kindly'

F*H
fāh adj. 'stained, tainted; hostile,
   criminal'
ġefeh/ġefeah 'rejoiced' *p.* ġefēgon
fēoh 'cattle, (movable) wealth'
   gen. fēos

fōh 'take!'
ġefeoht N. 'fight'
feoht-eð 'fights' *p.* feaht
fīht-wīte 'fine for fighting'
fǣhð F. 'hostility, feud'
fēhð 'he takes, holds, grabs' (fōn)

F*L
fela adj./subst.+*gen.* 'many'
fela– 'very-'
fell N. 'hide, skin'
feall-eð 'falls; dies' *p.* fēoll
fealu adj. 'tawny, muddy-coloured'
    gen. fealwes
fēol-eð 'adheres to; penetrates;
    departs'
fola m. 'foal'
fūl adj. 'foul, impure'
full adj. 'full, complete'
ġefyll 'downfall, death, slaughter'
ġefyll-að I 'fulfill; fill'
fyll-eð I 'fells, destroys'
fyllo F. 'fulness'
folc N. 'people, nation'
folc– 'public–'
ġefylce N. 'battalion'
feld M. 'open land, field'
folde f. 'earth'
fold– *pref.* 'earth-'
fyldon *ppl.* 'filled'; *pp.* (ā)fyld
folg-að 'follows, serves' *p.* folgode
folgoð M. 'following, retinue'
fylg-eð 'pursues, follows, practices'
fulluht M. 'baptism'
folm Fm. 'hand'
ġefǣlsod *pp.* 'purged'
fullǣst/fylst M. 'help, support'
fylst-eð 'helps' *p.* fyste
fultum M. 'help, aid'
fultum-að 'helps, aids' *p.* fultumede
fealw-að 'yellows, fades, ripens'
fealwes, etc. cf. fealu 'tawny'
fȳlð F. 'filth'

fylð = fealleð 'falls'
fulwiht 'baptism'

FL*
flēa 'flea(s)'
flōc 'a flatfish'
flōd M. 'flood; water'
flēog-eð 'flies' *ppl.* flugon
-floga '-flier'
flogettan 'to flutter'
flēah 'flew'; 'fled'
flyht M. 'flying, flight'
flîhð 'flees; puts to flight' (flēon)
flēam M. 'flight (in battle)'
ġefliem-eð 'puts to flight'
flān M. 'arrow'
flēon 'to flee; put to flight'
flōr 'floor, expanse, bed'
flȳs N. 'fleece, coat'
flǣsc N. 'flesh'
flett N. 'floor; living-space'
ġeflit N. 'a contention, dispute;
    strife'
flēot-að 'floats' *p.* flēat, fluton
flot N. 'sea'
flota m. 'boat; fleet; sailor'
aflote adj. 'afloat'
flot-here M. 'pirate force'
flot-mann M. 'sailor'
flōweð/flēwð 'flows' *p.* flēow

F*M
fāmiġ adj. 'foamy'
fǣmne f. 'maiden, woman'

F*N
fana M. 'banner'
fenn 'fen, marsh, moor'
fēon 'to hate'; 'to be glad'
fēond 'enemy' *pl.* fȳnd
ġefēonde *p.* 'rejoiced'; adj. 'joyful'
fand-að II 'tests, investigates'
find-eð/fint 'finds, discovers' *p.* fond

fund-að (tō) 'sets out for, strives for'
(ġe)feng M. 'grip, capture'
fēng p. 'he took, grabbed'
fengel M. 'prince, lord'
ġefangen pp. 'taken, caught'
onfongen pp. 'received, admitted'
finger M. 'finger'
fenix M. 'phoenix'

FN*
fnǣst M. 'a blowing, breathing'

F*R
fāra gen.pl. 'of foes'
far-eð/færð 'goes' p. fōr(on)
pp. ġefaren
fær M. 'peril, sudden danger'
fær– 'sudden-, unexpected-'
fær N. 'journey; locomotion'
pl. faru
fēr-eð 'goes, departs' p. fērde
fer-að 'ferries, brings' p. ferode
ġefēra m. 'comrade, companion'
fēara adj. gen. pl. 'of few'
feorr adj. 'far (away)'
feor-að 'proceeds'
fīras Mpl. 'people, humans'
fīer- 'four-'
fōr p. 'went' (faran)
fōr F. 'expedition'
for prep. 'before, on account of'
etc.
for– prefix often denoting a
destructive aspect
fore prep. 'in the presence of;
instead of'
fore– 'beforehand; very'
fȳr N. 'fire'
fyrr adv. 'further'
for-cuð adj. 'evil, despised'
āfǣred/āfȳrrde pp. 'frightened'
fierd F. '(general) army'

fierd-wîte 'penalty for avoiding
military service'
fērde p. 'went'
ford M. 'ford'
for-dēman I 'to condemn'
for-dōn 'to destroy, corrupt'
for-ġifan 'to grant, give over; forgive'
p. forġeaf
for-ġieldan 'to pay up, indemnify'
ferġen = ferian 'to carry'
firġen- 'mountain-'
for-ġeat 'forgot' pl. forġēaton
for-ġitolnes F. 'forgetfulness'
fearh M. 'piglet' gen. fēares
feorh MN 'life. soul' gen. fēores
for-habbað 'refrains, restrains from'
for-hāten pp. 'forsworn, false'
ferhð MN 'mind, soul'
ferhð-loca m. 'body'
for-hwî 'because'
forht adj. 'scared, timid'
fyrhto F. 'fright, dread'
forht-að II 'is scared, dreads'
ferhtlic adj. 'just, honest'
for-hwega adv. 'somewhat'
fǣrlic adj. 'sudden, unexpected'
ġefērlǣc-eð 'associates'
for-licġan 'to abandon'
færeld 'journey, expedition'
for-liġeð 'commits adultery'
fyrlen adj. 'remote'
for-liġer M.'adulterer'
for-lǣteð 'lets go, abandons; allows'
feorm F. 'provision, feast; rent'
feormað 'receives as a guest;
sustains; consumes; polishes'
forma adj. 'first, earliest'
fyrmest 'foremost, in the first place'
fearn N. 'fern'
feorran adv. 'from far back/off';
vb. 'to remove, distance'
fērend M. 'traveller'
firen F. 'a crime'

firen- 'wicked-, sinful-'
foran prep.+*dat.* 'before'
foran tō 'beforehand'
fȳren adj. 'fiery'
fyrn– 'far-off, long-ago'
fǣringa adv. 'suddenly, unexpectedly'
for-nēah adj. 'very near'
firen-lust M.'lustfulness'
for-nam *p.* 'deprived of, took away'
fēores *gen.* of feorh 'life'
feors-að 'proceeds; removes'
fyrs M. 'gorse-bush'
fersc adj. 'fresh'
ġefērscipe M. 'community, comradery'
for-sēah *p.* 'despised, renounced'
forst M. 'frost'
fyrst adj. 'first'
first MN 'a space of time'
fore-stihtung F. 'predestination'
fore-steall 'fine for robbery'
for-sewen *pp.* 'despised'
for-rotednes F. 'corruption'
faroð M. 'shore'
fǣrð 'goes'
ferð = ferhð 'spirit'
feorðe 'fourth'
forð adv. 'forwards, onwards etc'
    can = ferhð 'spirit, mind'
forð-ian 'to accomplish, progress with'
forðī 'because'
forð-fērde *p.* 'died'
forðōht *pp.* 'in despair'
forðǣm/forðon etc. conj./adv.
    'because, therefore'
furðum adv. 'just as, quite, further'
ferðan = furðum
forðenċeð 'mistrusts'; cf. forðoht
furðor adv. 'more distant'
furðr-að 'furthers, promotes'
forð-sīð M. 'going forth, death'
fore-weard adj. 'to the front, early'
for-wyrnan 'to prevent, to deny'
fyrwit N. 'curiosity, inquisitiveness'

FR*
frēa m. 'lord, esp. God'
frēo adj. 'free'
freċ adj. 'greedy, eager'
freca m. 'champion'
frēċedness F. 'danger'
fricgan 'to ask'
frēċne adj. 'dangerous, savage'
frēċennis 'danger'
fracoð adj. 'vile, contemptible'
ġefrēd-an 'to feel, sense'
frōd adj. 'wise'
frēod F. 'peace, goodwill'
frōfor F. 'help, consolation'
frēfrað 'gladdens, consoles'
frēfrend 'comforter e.g. the Holy
    Ghost'
ġefrǣġe N. 'hearing, knowledge,
    report'
frîġe *pl.* of frēo 'free'
friġeð 'asks' (fricgan)
frigneð 'enquires'
frēoliċ adj. 'free, free-born, generous'
frēols 'freedom, privilege; festival'
frēols-iað 'celebrate'
fram prep.+*dat.* 'from, by, arising
    from'
from adj. 'bold, energetic'
fruma m. 'beginning, origin'
frum– 'first-'
frem-ian II 'to benefit, help'
frem-eð I 'does, commits'
    pp. ġefremed
fremde adj. 'foreign, strange'
frumsceaft 'origin, Creation, the
    original condition'
fremsumnes F. 'kindness, generosity'
frum-stōl M. 'base, place of origin'
frymð MF 'start, origin'
frēan *gen.* of frēa 'lord'
frîn-eð 'enquires' *ppl.* frunon
ġefrunen *pp.* 'learned, heard of'
franca m. 'spear'

Franc-land   'France'
frēond   M. 'friend', *pl.* frȳnd
frēond-rǣden   F. 'intimacy'
frēondscipe   M. 'friendship'
frēoriġ   adj. 'icy'
freteð   'devours' *p.* frǣt
ġefrǣtwade   *pp.* 'adorned'
frǣtwa   *pl.* 'treasures, ornaments'
frið   M. 'peace, sanctuary'
ġefriðeð   'makes peace with, guards'

F*S

fēos   *gen.*of fēoh 'cattle, wealth'
fūs   adj. 'eager'
fisc   M. 'fish'
fisc(n)að   M. 'fishing'
fēa-sceaft   adj. 'destitute'
fiscere   M. 'fisherman'
fæst   adj. 'secure, firm'
fæst-eð   'fasts'
fæstliċ   adj. 'firm, reliable'
fæsten   N. 'stronghold'; 'fasting'
ġefæstnode   *p.* 'fixed'
befæstan   I 'to entrust, commit'
fōstor   M. 'sustenance, food'

F*T

fǣt   '(gold) plate'
fæt   N. 'vessel; bag' *pl.* fatu
fēt   'feeds'
fet-að   'to fetch' *p.* fetode
fētt   adj. 'fat'
fōt   M. 'foot' *pl.* fēt
fǣtels   M. 'vessel'
fetels   M. '(sword-)belt'

F*TH

fēð   'he takes' (fōn)
fēða   m. 'footsoldier'
fēðe–   'foot-'
fæðm   M. 'bosom; embrace; fathom'
feðer, fiðer   MN 'feather, *pl.* wing'
fiðer–   'winged-'; 'four-'

F*W

fēawe   adj.*pl.* 'few'
fēower   'four'
fēowertiġ   'forty'

F*X

fox   M. 'fox'
feax   N. 'hair'
fexede   *pp.* 'long-haired'
fix-að   'fishes'
fixas   M*pl.* 'fishes'
fixnoð   M. 'fishing'

G*

ġē   *pl.* 'you'
ġe   conj. 'and, also'
ġe–   pref. with verbs: = completion
    or action taken to conclusion
ġe–   pref. with nouns: = a group
gā   'go!'; gǣð 'goes'
ġēa   adv. 'yes'
ġēo   adv. 'formerly, of old, already'

G*C

ġēac   M. 'cuckoo'
ġeoc   N. 'yoke'
ġiċel   Mm. 'icicle'
ġēocend   'saviour'
ġēocor   adj. 'grim, sad'

G*D

gād   N. 'lack, need; goad, point'
ġid(d)   N. 'song, poem, tale'
gōd   adj. 'good'; also as subst:
    'goodness; a good person'
God   M. 'God'
godcund   adj. 'divine, holy'
ġyden   F. 'goddess'
gōdnes   F. 'goodness'
onġeader   adv. 'together'
ġegadere   adv. 'together'

gad(e)rað 'gathers, brings together'
  p. gaderode
gadertang adv. 'continuous'
god-spell N.'gospel'
god-webb 'expensive cloth'

G*F

ġif   conj. 'if'
ġifu   F. 'giving, gift; grace'
ġief-an 'to give' p. ġeaf, ġēafon
gafol   N. 'tribute, tax, interest on
         debt'
ġifol   adj. 'liberal, generous'
gafeluc 'spear, javelin'
ġeofon/ġyfen N. 'ocean'
ġifen   pp. 'given'
ġifende 'giving'
ġîfre   adj. 'greedy, hungry'
ġift   NF 'marriage-portion, dowry'
ġifeðe   adj. 'allotted, fated, granted'

G*G

ġegnum   adv. 'straight'
ġegnunga adv. 'instantly; clearly'
ġîgant   M. 'giant'
gag(ā)tes 'agate; jet'
ġeoguð   F. 'youth; youngsters'

G*L

gāl   N. 'lust, levity';
         adj.'promiscuous'
gal-eð   'sings, chants' p. gōl
gǣl-eð   'hinders'
ġēol(a) 'Yule'
ġeolu   adj. 'yellow' gen. ġeolwes
gōl   p. 'sang, chanted'
ġyl-eð   'yells'
ġeol(e)ca m. 'yolk'
onġeald p. 'paid for'
ġi(e)ld N. 'compulsory payment;
         offering, sacrifice; idol'
ġield-an 'to pay over' ppl. guldon
gold   N. 'gold'

gylden   adj. 'golden'
galdor   N. 'song, charm, spell'
         pl. galdru
gold-wine M. 'gold-friend, patron'
ġealga   m. 'gallows; cross'
ġielp   MN 'boasting, pride, vanity'
ġielp-eð 'boasts' p. ġealp
gǣlsa   m. 'pride, luxury'
gylt   M. 'guilt, offence'
ġeolwað 'becomes yellow'

GL*

glîu   = glîw 'mirth'
glad-að 'gladdens; rejoices; shines'
         p. gladode
glæd   adj. 'glad' dat.pl. gladum
glēd   F. 'glowing coal, fire'
glîd-eð 'glides, slips' p. glād glidon
glōf   F. 'glove'
glōma   m. 'twilight'
ġeglengde pp. 'adorned'
glîdeð/glît 'glides'
glæs   N. 'glass, glass vessel' pl. glasu
glitnian II 'to glitter, sparkle'
glēaw   adj. 'clever, perspicacious'
glîw   N. 'glee, fun; music'
glîw-man M. 'singer (etc)'

G*M

ġim   M. 'gem, jewel' pl. ġimmas
ġîem-eð 'cares for, pays attention'
guma   m. 'man'
gamol   adj. 'aged, greying'
gamen   N. 'sport, amusement, game'
ġȳmen   F. 'concern, care'
ġēomrung F. 'grief'
gum-ċyst F. 'generosity'
ġēom(o)r adj. 'sad, depressing'
ġēomrode p. 'lamented'

G*N

gān	'to go'
ā-gān	*pp.* 'gone by, passed'
ġe-gān	'to conquer'
be-gān	'to practice, enact'
on-gan	*p.* 'began'
ġēn	adv. 'yet, still, further, besides'
onġēan	prep/adv. 'opposite'
ġîn-að	'yawns, gapes'
ginn	adj. 'spacious'
ġeond	prep.+acc. 'throughout, over'
ġeond–	'throughout, thoroughly, too much–'
ġin-fæst	adj.'liberal'
ġeong	adj. 'young'
gang	M. 'travel; something travelling; circuit'
gang-an	'to go' *p.* gang/gong
genga	m. 'goer'
gang-dagas	M*pl.* 'Rogation days'
ġeoniende	'gaping'
ganot	M. 'gannet'

GN*

gnîdan	'to crumble (something)'
gnorn	adj. 'sad, depressed'; also subst. 'grief'
gnornode	*p.* 'mourned, lamented'

G*P

ġēap	adj. 'spacious, broad'
ġeapsis	'jasper'

G*R

gār	M. 'spear'
ġēar	NM. 'year'
ġēar–	'yore-; olden'
ġēara	adv. 'of old'
ġeare	adv. = ġearwe 'thoroughly'
ġearo	adj. 'prepared, ready'
	gen. ġearwes
ġier-eð	'readies'
ġearcian	II 'to prepare, get'

ġeard	M. 'yard, residence'
ġierede	*p.* 'readied'
ġyrd	F. 'yard, rod'
beġyrdan	I 'to encase, enlose, surround'
ġirela	m. 'dress, outfit'
ġe-arn	= arn 'ran'
gurron	*ppl.* 'groaned, creaked'
ġyrnde	*p.* 'yearned (for)' +*gen.*
ġeorn	adj.+*gen.* 'eager (for)'
ġeorne	adv. 'keenly, properly'
gærs	N. 'grass'
gār-secg	M.'ocean; ?Neptune'
ġyrstan-dæġ	'yesterday'
ġearwa	F*pl.* 'gear, equipment'
ġearwe	adv. 'thoroughly, well, fully'
	cf. ġearo adj.
ġearwian	II 'to prepare, clothe, equip'

GR*

Grēcas	M*pl.* 'the Greeks'
grēcisc	adj. 'Greek'
grædiġ	adj. 'greedy'
graf-eð	'digs up; engraves' *p.* grōf
græf	N. 'cave, grave'
græġ	adj. 'grey'
gram	adj. 'fierce, threatening'
grem-að	'provokes, annoys"
grîma	m. 'mask, helmet'
grim(m)	adj. 'fierce, terrible'
grim-eð	'rages'
grom	= gram ('angry')
grymetiġeð	I 'roars, bellows'
grēne	adj. 'green'
grēn-að	II 'turns green'
grîn	NF 'snare, noose'
grind-eð	'grates, grinds' *ppl.* grundon
grund	M. 'ground, bottom'
grundlēas	adj. 'bottomless'
grundstān	M. 'foundation'
grāp	M. 'grip'
grāpað	II 'seizes'

grîpeð   'grips, seizes' *p.* ġegrāp
     pp. ġegripen
gryre   M.'a horror, a cause of terror;
     roughness, violence'
grorn   adj. 'sad'; subst. 'sorrow'
græs   N. 'grass' *pl.* grasu
grisliċ   adj. 'grisly, horrible'
grēt-eð/grēt 'salutes, greets' *p.* grētte
grēat   adj. 'big'
grēot   N. 'grit, sand, earth'
grēot-eð   'weeps'
grið   N. 'truce, guarantee of safety'
grōweð/grēwð   'grows' *p.* grēow
     pp. grōwen

G*S

gōs   F. 'goose' *pl.* gēs
ġēse   'yes'
ġîsl   M. 'hostage'
gās-rîċ   'powerful beast'
gāst   M. 'spirit, soul; supernatural
     force'
gast/ġiest M. 'guest, stranger'
gāstliċ   adj. 'spiritual, holy'
ġystren-   'yester-'

G*T

gāt   F. 'she-goat'
ġeat   N. 'gate, opening' *pl.* gatu
ġēot-eð   'pours out, gushes'
ġît/ġîeta adv. 'still, yet'
ġit   pron. 'you two'
-ġiet-eð   'gets, etc' *p.* -ġeat -ġēaton
Gota   *pl.*-n 'Goth(s)'
ġyte   m. 'outpour, flow'
ġeatoliċ adj. 'magnificent'
ġîtsung F. 'avarice, greed'
ġîtsere M. 'miser'
ġeatwe F*pl.* 'arms, war-gear'

G*TH

gǣð   'goes' *p.* gang
gūð   F. 'combat, war'

H*

hū   adv. 'how'
hē   'he'
hēa   = hēah 'high'
hēo   'she; they'
hî, hîe   *nom./acc.* 'they'; *acc.* 'her'

H*B

habbað   'have' *p.* hæfdon
hæbbe   subj. 'might have'
hebbeð   'raises, lifts' *p.* hōf

H*C

hycgan   'think, consider etc' *p.* hogode

H*D

hād M. 'state, condition, rank, order'
–hād   'condition of –'
ġehād-od *pp.* 'in religious orders'
hēd-eð   +*gen.* 'heeds, observes' *ppl.*
     hēddon
behȳd   *pp.* 'hidden'
hȳd   'hide, skin'
hȳd-an   'to hide something; to tie with
     a hide rope'; *ppl.* hȳddon
hȳdiġ   = hyġdiġ 'thoughtful'
hādor   adj. 'clear, bright'; subst.
     'clearness'
hider   adv. 'hither'

H*F

hæf   N. 'ocean'
hæf-ð   *pl.* hafað 'has, possesses'
     ppl. hæfdon
hef-eð   'raises'
hēaf   M. 'wailing'
hēof-eð   'laments' *p.* hēof
hōf   *pl.* hōfon 'raised'
hōf   M. 'hoof'

hof   N. 'court, hall'
hȳf   F. 'hive'
hafoc   M. 'hawk'
hēafod   N. 'head' *gen.* hēafdes
hēafod-   as pref: 'capital-, chief etc'
behēafdian   II 'to behead'
hefiġ   adj. 'heavy, serious'
hefigod   *pp.* 'weighed down'
hafela   m. 'head'
hafen-að   II 'grasps, brandishes'
hæfen   F. 'harbour, haven'
(ā)hæfen/hafen   *pp.* 'raised, lifted up'
heofon   M. 'heaven(s)'
hafenlēas   adj. 'destitute'
hæft   M. 'fetter'; adj. 'captive'
ġehæfted   *pp* 'chained, captured'
hæfð   'has, possesses' (habban)

H*G

haga   m. 'hedge, enclosure'
ġehæġ   N. 'field, meadow'
hiġ   = hî 'they; them'
hyġe   M. 'thought; mind, attitude'
hyġ-eð   'thinks about' (hycgan)
hogode   'thought of, was busy with'
    (hogian)
hyġd   FN 'mind'
hyġdiġ   adj. 'thoughtful, nice'
hagol   MN 'hail'
hagosteald   adj./subst 'unmarried,
    of military age'

H*H

hēah   adj. 'high; deep'
hēah-   'chief, arch-, great'
ġehōh   'hang, suspend!'
hēhst/hȳhst   adj. 'highest'
hēhst   'hangs up'
hēht   'is called; orders'
hyht   MF 'hope, trust'
hēhðo   F. 'height; the heavens'

H*L

hāl   adj. 'healthy, whole'
hæl-eð   I 'cures, heals'
hælu/hæl   F. 'health, salvation'
hæle   M. 'man'
hell/helle   Ff. 'Hell'
hel-eð   'conceals'
heall   F. 'hall, palace'
hol   adj. 'hollow'; subst. 'a cave'
hēaliċ   adj. 'exalted, noble'
ġehealdsumnes   F. 'custom; fast'
hild   F. 'warfare, combat'
(ā)hild   *pp.* 'bent, laid down'
hold   adj. 'loyal, friendly'
hyldu   F. 'favour, kind notice'
healdeð   'holds, possesses, contains'
    p. heold
heldeð   'inclines, leans'
healf   F. 'half; side'
heolfer   N. 'gore'
hālga   adj. 'holy'; subst. 'saint'
hāliġ   adj. 'holy'
ġehālgod   *pp.* 'hallowed, saintly'
helm   M. 'cover, lid, helmet, crown
    of a tree; protector, leader'
helm-að   'covers'
helma   m. 'helm, rudder'
holm   M. 'sea'
Hælend   M. 'Saviour i.e. Christ'
help   FM 'help'
help-eð/hilpð   'helps'
huilpe   f. 'sea-bird, curlew'
heals   M. 'neck; prow'
healsað   'implores'
heolstor   M. 'darkness, invisibility'
hilt   M. 'hilt'
holt   M. 'forest, wood'
hylt   'holds; leans'
hæleð   M. 'man, hero'
hāl-wende   adj. 'salutary'

HL*

hlēo = hlēow 'shelter'
hlad-eð 'he loads, draws' p. hlēod,
hlād(on) pp. ġehlæden
hlid-on ppl. 'they arose, appeared'
hlūd adj. 'loud, noisy'
hlȳdeð 'is noisy'
hlǣder F. 'ladder'
hlāf M. 'loaf'
hlǣfdiġe F. 'lady, woman of status'
hlāford M. 'lord'
hlifað II 'towers up'
ā-hlōg p. 'laughed'
hleahtor M.'laughter'
hlimman I 'to resound'
hlinað 'leans, reclines' p. hlynode
hlyneð 'shouts' p. hlynede
be-hlǣneð 'surrounds'
hlynsode p. 'echoed, resounded'
hlēapeð 'leaps' p. hlēop
hlēor N. 'cheek, face'
hlîsa m. 'sound; reputation'
hlæst N. 'load, cargo'
hlēotan 'to cast lots; get, obtain'
ppl.hluton
hlott N. '(selection by) lot, portion'
hlūt(t)or adj. 'bright, clear'
hlið N. 'cliff, slope' pl. hleoðu
hlōð F. 'crowd, troop; booty'
hlēoðor N. 'noise; voice'
hlēoðrode p. 'spoke'
hlǣw MN '(burial) mound, hill'
hlēow MN 'shelter, refuge'

H*M

hām M. 'home, household, village'
hamm M. 'pasture-land, water-land'
hama m. 'coating, cover, 'skin''
him '(to) him, them'
hǣmed N. 'sexual intercourse,
adultery' pl. hǣmedru

H*N

hēan adj. 'lowly, pitiful'
hēan/hēanne = hēah 'high'
henn F. 'hen'
hîen-eð 'humiliates' p. hȳnde
hōn 'to hang [someone]'
hancrēd M. 'cockcrow'
hand/hond F. 'hand; ownership,
position etc'
ġehende +dat 'close, handy'
(ġe)hend-eð 'catches'
hind F. 'female deer, hind'
hund M. 'hound, dog'
hund N. 'a hundred'
hund– prefix of numbers between 60
and 120
hond-bred 'palm'
hinder adj./adv. 'after, behind, back'
hundred N. '100; a local court'
hond-ġesella m. 'companion'
hin-fūs adj. 'keen to get away'
hang-að 'hangs, dangles; hangs
someone' p. heng
pp. ġehangen
hunig N. 'honey'
hungor M. 'hunger'
hungrig adj. 'hungry'
hēanlic adj. 'humiliating'
heonon adv. 'hence'
hēaness F. 'highness'
hin-sîð M. 'going hence, death'
hent-an 'to pursue; lay hold of'
hunta m. 'huntsman'
hunt(n)oð M. 'hunting'
huntēontiġ 'one hundred'
hîenð(u) F. 'humiliation'

HN*

hine acc. 'him'
hnǣġed pp. 'humbled, vanquished'
hnîġeð 'bends, bows' pp. hniġen
hnol M. 'top of head'
hnipað 'bends/inclines the head'

hnesce adj. 'soft, mild; enervated'
ġehnǽst N. 'conflict'
hnîtan 'to gore, clash' *ppl.* hniton
hnutu F. 'nut'

H*P

hēap MF 'crowd, band'
hop N. 'swampy area'
hop-að 'hopes, trusts in'
hōpiġ adj. 'bouncy'

H*R

hār adj. 'grey & ancient'
hara m. 'hare'
hēr adv. 'here'
here M. 'raiding army' *dat.* herġe
her-eð I 'praises' (herian)
hēore adj. 'agreeable'
heora 'their, of them'
heoru M. 'sword'
hire/hyre 'hers, to her'
hîerra adj. 'higher, superior'
hūru adv. 'however, yet'
hȳr-eð I 'hears, listens to, obeys'
ġehȳr-að I 'obeys'
heard adj. 'hard, stern'
hîred M. 'household, group'
hord *gen.* -es 'treasure-hoard'
hyrde M. 'shepherd'
heard mōd adj. 'bold; obstinate'
heriġe *obl.* of here 'army'
hǣring M. 'herring'
hord-ern N. 'treasury, store-room'
hærfest M. 'harvest-time, autumn'
heriġean 'to praise'
herg-að 'raids'
hergung F. 'pillage'
here-ġeatu 'war-tax'
heoro-hōcyht adj. 'fiercely barbed'
hearm M. 'injury, damage'
horn M. 'musical or drinking horn'
hyrned *pp.* 'horned'
hearpe f. 'harp'

hors N. 'horse' *pl.* hors
horsc adj. 'sharp, cunning'
ġehȳrsum +*dat.* 'obedient'
ġehorsian II 'to provide with horses'
hyrst F. 'decoration, article of value'
heorte f. 'heart, disposition'
heorot M. 'hart, stag'
here-toga m. 'general, consul'
heorð M. 'hearth; home'

HR*

hrā = hrǣw 'corpse, body'
hrycg M. 'spine, ridge'
hreddan 'to rescue'
hrǣd adj. 'quick, alert'
   dat.pl. hradum
hrǣdlîce adv. 'quickly'
ġehroden *pp.* 'adorned'
hrēof adj. 'rough, scaley'
hrōf M. 'roof, ceiling'
hrefn M. 'raven'
hrǣġl N. 'clothing; armour'
hrēoh adj. 'rough, fierce, stormy'
hrēam M. 'alarm, outcry'
hrîm M. 'rime, hoar-frost'
hrîem-eð 'shouts'
hrēmiġ adj. 'boastfull'
hremming F. 'obstacle'
hremmas M*pl.* 'ravens'
hrān M. 'reindeer'; *p.* 'he touched'
hrēone *acc.*M. of hrēoh 'rough'
hrîn-eð 'touches' *p.* hrān
hron/hran M. 'whale'
hrinde adj. 'hoary'
hring M. 'ring, circuit'
hrepsung 'evening'
hrōpende 'yelling' *ppl.* hrēopon
hrēran 'to shake' *ppl.* hrērdon
hrōr adj. 'active, agile'
hruron *ppl.* 'fell down'; *pp.* ġehroren
hryre M. 'fall, ruin'
hrǣs *gen.* of hrēaw 'corpse'

hrēos-eð/hrēst/hrīst 'sinks, falls down'
   p. hrēas
hrūse   f. 'earth, ground'
hrysted   *pp.* = hyrsted 'decorated'
hraðe   adv. 'quickly, promptly'
hrēð   MN 'victory'
–hrēðiġ   'exultant'
hreðer   M. 'breast; heart, mind'
hrīðer   N. 'ox, bull etc'
hraðost   superl. 'quickest'
hrǣw/hrēaw   'corpse' *gen.* hrǣs
hrēow   F. 'sorrow, repentance'
hrēowsian   II 'to repent'

H*S

hās   adj. 'hoarse'
hasu   adj. 'grey, ash-coloured'
hǣs   F. 'request'
his   'his, of him; its, of it'
hūs   N. 'house'
hys   = his/is
hyse   M. 'son, young man' *pl.* hyssas
hūsc/hūx   N. 'scorn, ridicule'
hūsel   N. 'the host (Holy
   Communion)'
hosp   M. 'abuse, insult'
hǣst   adj. 'violent'
haswiġ-   'grey-' *cf.* hasu

H*T

hāt   adj. 'hot'
hātte   'is called'
hāt-að   'heats up'
hāt-eð   'is called; orders'
hat-að   II 'hates'
hǣt-eð   'heats'
hǣtt   *p.* 'ordered'
hǣtu   F. 'heat'
hēte   *p.* 'you commanded'; hēt 'he
   commanded'
hete   M. 'hate'
hīt   'hides' (hȳdan)
hit   'it'

hāt-heort   adj. 'passionate, angry'
hatol/hetol   adj. 'hostile'
hetelīċe   adv. 'hatefully, violently'
ġehāten   *pp.* '(is) called; ordered'
hatung   F. 'hatred'

H*TH

hǣð   N. 'heathland'
heaðo–/heaðu–   pref. 'war, battle'
hūð   F. 'booty, quarry'
hȳð   F. 'harbour, landing-place'
hȳðan   'to plunder'
hǣðen   adj. 'heathen'

H*W

hāw-að   II 'gazes on, notices'
hēow   *p.* 'cut down' *pp.* ġehēawen
hīw/, hēow   N. 'colour; appearance,
   type'
hīwan   *pl.* 'members of family,
   household'
hīw-að   'fashions, forms' *p.* hēowade
   pp. ġehīwod
hǣwen   adj. 'bluish, purply'

HW*

hwā   'who, what; anyone'
ġehwā   'every(one)'
hwȳ   'why'
ġehwǣde   adj. 'insignificant'
hwider   'whither'
hwæl   M. 'whale' *pl.* hwalas
hwēol   N. 'wheel'
hwīl   F. 'a time, a while'
hwelċ/hwilċ   'which; whatever'
ġehwilċ   'each, every'
hwealf   F. 'arch, vault'   also adj.
hwīlum/hwīlon   adv. 'sometimes'
hwelpas   *pl.* 'cubs'
hwamm/hwemm   M. 'corner'
hwǣm   *dat.* of hwā
hwēne   adv. 'a little'
hwōn   adj./subst. 'a little'

35

hwon   'by which'; tō hwon/for hwon
        'for what, why'
hwonne/hwænne 'when'
hwanon 'whence'
hwēop   p. 'threatened'
hwǽr   'where'; ġehwǽr 'everywhere'
hwearf p. 'turned'
hwyrfð/hwearfað' revolves, exists,
            changes'
hwurfon/hwearfodon ppl. 'turned'
hwǽs   'whose'
hwistlung F. 'whistling, hissing'
hwæt   'what!: what...?'
hwæt   adj. 'bold, active'
hwǽte   M. 'wheat'
hwet-eð 'whets, incites; is keen'
hwît   adj. 'white, bright'
hwæthwugu 'somewhat'
-hwatan pl. suff. 'heroes'
hweoðu F. 'breeze'
hwæðer 'whether'; ġehwæðer 'both'
hwæðere adv. 'nonetheless, yet'
hweowul N. 'wheel'

H*X
huxlîce adv. 'degradingly'

L*
la   'lo!'
lēo   Mm. 'lion'

L*B
libban 'to live' p. lifede
lyb-lāc MN 'magic, spellwork'

L*C
lāc-eð 'vibrates, makes play with;
            flies'
lāc   N. 'sacrifice, offering'
ġelāc   N. 'play; chaos; offering'
lacu   F. 'stream, pond'
lǽċe   M. 'doctor'
lǽċ-eð 'captures'

lēac   N. 'plant, herb; leek'
lîċ   N. 'body; corpse'
lîc-að +dat. 'it pleases someone'
ġelîċ   adj. 'like, similar to' +dat.
ġelîca subst. 'an equal, a similar'
ġelîċe adv. 'likewise'
-liċ, lîċe etc (suffix) 'like; -ly'
lōc-ian 'look, gaze'; p. lōcade
loca   m. 'closed place;stronghold'
lȳc-ð   'shuts or locks up; excludes':
        pp. locen
lǽcedom M. 'healing'
lecgan 'to lay, position, arrange'
liċgan 'to lie down, be at rest, extend'
lîc-hama m. 'body, bodily shell'
lîchamliċ adj. 'physical'
lācn-að II 'heals, cures'
lācnung F. 'healing, remedy'
ġelîcnyss F. 'likeness'
anlîcost adj. +dat. 'most like (to)'

L*D
lād   F. 'course, way, street'
lǽd-eð 'leads, brings' p. lǽdde,
            lǽddon
lead   N. 'lead (metal)'
lēod   M. 'man'
lēode   Fpl. 'nation, people'
lēod–   'of one's country; general '
lid   N. 'ship'
lida   m. 'sailor'
lǽden   'Latin'
Lǽdenware Mpl. 'the Romans'
lid-mon M. 'sailor'
ġeliden pp. 'sailed, travelled'
(h)loden pp. 'laden'
(h)lǽdder F. 'ladder'
lādðēow = lāttēow 'leader'

L*F
lāf   F. 'remnant, remains'
lǽf-eð 'leaves behind, bequeaths'
        p. lǽfde

lēf   adj. 'feeble, precarious'
lēf   *pl.* 'loaves'
lēaf   M. 'leaf'
lēaf   F. 'permission'
ġelēafa   m. 'faith, belief'
lēof   adj. 'dear, beloved'
leof-að   'lives' *p.* leofede
līf   N. 'life'
līef-eð   'allows, entrusts' *p.* (ā)lȳfde
(ġe)līef-eð/ġelȳfð   'believes';
    sim. belīefeð
lof   N. 'praise'
lufu   Ff. 'love'
luf-að   'loves' *p.*lufode
(ā)lēfed   *pp.* 'injured, ill'
ġelȳfed   adj. 'advanced in age'
līf-dagas   M*pl.* 'lifetime'
lifi(ġ)ende   'living'
lyft   'air, atmosphere, sky'

L*G
lagu   F. 'water'
læġ   'lay' *pl.* lǣgon
lēag   *p.* 'lied';'lent'
lēog-an   'to lie, betray, deceive'
līġ/lēġ   MN 'fire; lightning'
leġ-eð   'lays' (lecgan)
liġ-eð   'lies, reclines' (licgan)
ġelōg-að   II 'arranges; lodges'
leġer   N. 'bed, repose; grave'
līġet(u)   'lightning'

L*H
lah–   'law-'
ġelæht   *pp.* 'caught'
leahte   *p.* 'moistened'
lēoht   N. 'light'; also adj. 'light'
līht-eð   'lightens; illuminates'
līhting   F. 'illumination'
leahtor   M. 'vice, sin'
leahtriċ   M. 'lettuce'

L*L
lilie   f. 'lily'
(be)leolc   *p.* 'made sway' (lācan)

L*M
lām   N. 'clay, earth'
lēoma   *pl.*-n m. 'gleam, light'
līm   M. 'sticky lime; trap'
lim   N. 'limb (of a tree etc)
    pl. leomu
ġelōma   m. 'tool'
ġelōme   adj./adv. 'often, frequent(ly)'
ġelimpeð   'happened, came about'
    p. ġelomp *pp.* ġelumpen
ġelimpliċ   adj. 'appropriate'

L*N
lǣne   adj. 'temporary, transient,
    perishable, frail'
lēan   N. 'reward'
lēan-ian   'to reward'
lēon   *obl.* 'lion'; sim. lēona
līne   f. 'line'
linn-an   'to lose' +*dat.*
lencten   M. 'springtime'
lind   M. '(linden-wood) shield'
lond/land   N. 'land'
Lunden-byriġ   F. 'london'
lange   adv. 'for a long time'
ġelang   adj. 'dependent'
leng   F. 'length, height'
leng/lencg   adv. 'longer'
ġeleng-an   'to protract'
lang-fǣre   adj. 'long-enduring'
lungre   adv. 'quickly'
langsum   adj. 'lasting, tedious'
līnsēd   'linseed'
lent/lendeð   'lands/ends up, goes'

L*P
lopystran   f.*pl.* 'lobsters'

L*R

lār   F. 'learning; advice'
lǣr-eð   'teaches' p. lǣrde
(tō) lore   'to the end, to destruction'
ġelǣred   adj. 'educated'
(for)loren   pp. 'lost'
leorn-ian   'learnt, studied' p. leornode
leornung   F. 'learning'
leorneras   Mpl. 'disciples; scholars'
lārēow   M. 'teacher'

L*S

lǣs   adv. 'less'; þȳ lǣs þe 'lest'
lǣssa   adj. 'less, smaller'
lēas   adj. 'false'; +gen. 'free (of)'
–lēas   'without'
(ā)līes-eð   'releases' pp. lȳsed
liss   F. 'grace, kindness'
losian   'to fail, die; escape'
lēasung   F. 'lie, fiction'
lēasere   M. 'liar, hypocrite'
lāst   M. 'foot-print, track'
lǣst   superl. 'least'
lǣst-eð   'achieves, carries out, endures'
list   'skill, cleverness'
lust   M. 'desire'
lyst-eð   'it pleases someone (to…)'
lustbǣre   adj. 'desirable, pleasant'
lustlīċe   adv. 'willingly'
lustum   adv. 'gladly'
lǣswe   obl. 'pasture'

L*T

lǣt   'he leads; he left'
lǣt-an   'to allow, permit; leave behind,
     let out' p. lēt
onlǣt-an   'to relax (something)'
forlǣt-eð   'abandons'
læt   adj. 'late, tardy'
lett-an   'to hinder, impede' ppl. letton
lot   N. 'trickery'
lūt-an   'to bend, bow'
lūt-ian   II 'to lie hidden, lurk'

lytiġ   adj. 'cunning'
lȳtel   adj. 'little'
lȳtl-að   II 'lessens, shortens'
(ā)lȳten   pp. 'bent over'
lator, latost   adj. 'later… latest'
(h)lūtt(o)r   adj. 'clear'
lāttēow   M. 'leader'

L*TH

lāð   adj./subst. 'loathesome, nasty'
lað-að   II 'invites'
lēoð   N. 'song, poem'
līðe   adj. 'gentle, sweet'
līð-eð/līð   'travels, sails'
līð   'lies down' (= liġeð)
lið   N. 'limb' pl. leoðu
līðiġað   'softens, calms'
ġelaðung   F. 'community'
leðer   M. 'leather'
lȳðre   adj. 'wicked, corrupt'

L*W

lǣwede   adj. 'lay (man)'

L*X

leax   'salmon' pl. -as
līx-eð   'shines' p. līxte

M*

ma   adj./adv. 'more'
mē   acc./dat. 'me, to me'

M*C

mac-að   II 'makes' p. macode
ġemæcca   'mate, match' pl. -n
mēċe   'sword'
meċ   acc. 'me'
mæcg   M. 'man; son'
miċel   adj. 'great, much'
miċlade   p. 'increased'
miċlum   adv. 'greatly'

M*D

mǣd   F. 'meadow' *pl.* mǣd(w)a
mēd   F. 'reward'
medu   'mead' *gen.* medwes
mid   prep. '(together) with, among,
   by'; mid þām þe 'when, while'
midde   adj./subst. 'middle'
mōd   N. 'mind, disposition, courage'
ofer-mōd   'pride, overconfidence'
mōdiġ   adj. 'haughty, brave'
mōdiġ(i)an   'to become proud;
   be brave; show anger'
mōd-ġeþanc   M. 'thought, mind'
mādmas   *pl.* = māðmas 'treasures'
medeme, medemliċ, medmiċel   adj.
   'middling, average'
onmiddan/onmiddum   'in the
   middle of'
midl   N. 'middle, centre'
medmiċel   adj. 'moderate'
mǣden   N. 'maiden'
middan-ġeard   M. 'the world'
mōdor   F. 'mother' *dat.* mēder
mōd-sefa   m. 'heart, mind'
medtrumnes   F. 'weakness, disability'
medwes   *gen.* of medu   'mead'

M*G

māga   m. 'son'
mago   M. 'son, kinsman' *pl.* mǣcgas
mǣġ   M. 'kinsman, relation'
   pl. māgas
mæġ   'he can' *pl.* magon
mæġden   N. 'maiden'
meagol   adj. 'strong, determined,
   confident'
magon   'they can'
mæġen   N. 'strength, power; a troop'
mæġen–   'huge, mighty–'
magister   M. 'master'
mǣġð   F. 'clan, race'
mæġð   F. 'maiden, wife'

mæġðhād   M. 'virginity'
mǣġ-wlite   M. 'form, species'

M*H

ġemāhliċ   adj. 'impudent' (= ġemāgliċ)
miht/meaht   F. 'power, force'
mihte/meahte   *p.* 'might, could'
   pl. meahton
mihtiġ   adj. 'mighty, important'

M*L

mǣl   N. 'mark, sign (e.g. cross);
   time, occasion'
mǣl-eð   'speaks, talks' *p.* mǣlde
mîl   F. 'a mile'
meolc   F. 'milk'
meld-ode   *p.* 'announced, proclaimed'
milde   adj. 'merciful, considerate'
molde   f. 'soil; the earth'
mylen   'mill'; –hwēowul 'millwheel'
mealt   *p.* 'melted' *pl.* multon
milts   F. 'compassion'

M*N

mān   N. 'crime'
mān–   'evil-'
ġemāna   m. 'community,
   communication'
man(n)   M. 'human, man' *pl.* men
man   'one' in 'one likes to...' etc.
ġeman   *pl.* ġemunon +*gen.* 'considers,
   remembers' *p.* ġemunde
ġemǣne   adj. 'in common'
unġemǣn   adj. 'unusual'
mǣn-eð   I 'means, signifies; mentions;
   bemoans'
mîn   adj. 'my, mine'
mōna   m. 'the moon'
mon-að   II 'urges' *p.* monade
myne   M. 'affection, feeling'
myn-að   'intends, aims to, considers'
   p. mynte
munuc   M. 'monk'

moncyn N. 'mankind'
mancus M. 'silver coin'
munuchād M. 'monastic order'
ġemanode p. 'instructed, encouraged'
mund F. 'hand; protector, protection'
ġemunde p. 'remembered'
gemynd N. 'thought, mind; memory'
ġemynde/ġemyndiġ adj. 'mindful (of)'
mundbora m. 'protector, officer'
ġemyndgað II 'remembers'
mānful adj. 'wicked'
ġemang N. 'mixture; multitude'
ġemeng-ed pp. 'mixed'
moniġ/maniġ adj. 'many'
menigo, mængeo F. 'crowd, host'
maniġfeald adj. 'various'
mennisc adj. 'human'
mynster N. 'monastery, minster'
mynsterliċ adj. 'monastic'
munt M. 'mountain'
mynte p. 'intended, aimed to'
man-þwǣre adj. 'gentle, merciful'
mōnað/mōnð M. 'month' pl. mōnðas

M*R
māra adj. 'greater, more'
mǣre adj. 'famous'
mǣr-eð 'glorifies; delimits'
ġemǣre N. 'boundary; territory'
mēra gen.pl. of mearh ('horse')
mere M. 'sea; lake'
mōr M. 'moor, morass'
mȳre f. 'a mare'
mearc F. 'mark, boundary, area'
myrce adj. 'murky'
mearg/mearh M. 'a horse' gen. mēares
myrġe adj. 'pleasant'
morġen M. 'morning; tomorrow'
meregrotan pl. 'pearls'
mearh – see mearg, above
marmor-stān M. 'marble'
murn-an, myrn-ð 'to mourn'
mǣrs-að II 'praises, exalts'

mēares - see mearg
mersc M. 'marsh'
mere-swȳn N. 'porpoise, dolphin'
martirdom M. 'martyrdom'
morð(or) M. 'murder, grave crime'
myrġð F. 'mirth, pleasure'
mǣrðu F. 'marvel, glory'

M*S
mæsse f. 'mass (holy communion)'
mis– 'wrongly, mis-'
muscle f. 'mussel'
misdǣd F. 'misdeed'
muslan = musclan 'mussels'
misliċ adj. 'unalike, varied'
missenliċ adj. 'various'
missēr M. 'a season'
mǣst adj./adv. 'most'
mæst M. 'mast'
ġemǣst pp. 'fattened up'
-mest '-most'
mist M. 'mist'
mōste mōston p. 'they might, were
      allowed to'
must M. 'raw wine'
mǣstling N. 'brass'

M*T
ġemǣte adj. 'suitable'
ġemǣtte p. 'came in dream'
ġemǣte adj. 'small'
mǣt p. 'measured'
mēt-eð I 'meet, come across'
met-eð 'measures out'; sim. āmetan
āmet pp. 'painted, studded'
mete, mǣte M. 'food' pl. mettas
ġemet adj. 'appropriate'; subst. 'a
      measure(ment)'
mitte (ðe) 'when, while'
mōt pl. mōton; 'may, is allowed to'
(ġe)mōt N. 'moot, judicial assembly;
      encounter'

me(o)tod 'God (as regulator of the
　　universe)'
ġemetfæst adj. 'reasonable'
metg-að 'moderates, controls,
　　restrains' p. metgode
ġemetgung F. 'moderation'
ġemetlīċe adv. 'moderately'
Metend 'God (as layer-out of the
　　universe)'

M*TH
mēð/mǣð F. 'rate, proportion; right-
　　ness, capability'
mēðe adj. 'tired'
mīð-eð 'hides, avoids'
mūð M. 'mouth'
mæðel N. 'council, discussion'
mæðel-að 'speaks out' p. maðelode
māð(u)m M. 'treasure, precious object'

M*W
māw-an 'to mow'
mēaw/mǣw M. 'seagull'
mēowle f. 'woman'

M*X
max N. 'net'
meox N. 'dung, dirt'

N*
nā/nō adv. 'not, not at all'
ne adv. 'not'; conj. 'nor'
nū adv. 'now'

N*B
nabb-an, nabbað 'not to have, to lack'
　　p. næfde
nebb N. 'bill, beak'

N*C
naca m. 'boat'
niċ 'not I'
nacod adj. 'naked'
nicor M. 'water-spirit or monster'
　　pl. nicras

N*D
nēod F. 'desire, zeal'
nēde adv. 'necessarily'
nēad-að/nīed-eð 'compels'
nīed FN. 'necessity, compulsion'
nīed-behēfe adj. 'necessary'
nēod-fracu F. 'greed'
nǣdl F. 'needle'
nēodlīċe adv. 'eagerly'
nǣdre f. 'adder, snake'
nīed-ðearf F. 'necessity; lack'

N*F
nafu F. 'nave (of a wheel)'
naf-að/næfð 'has not' p. næfde
nefa m. 'nephew, cousin'
nafola m. 'navel'
nǣfre adv. 'never'

N*G
ġenōg adj. 'enough'
ġenǣġed pp. 'attacked'
næġl M. 'nail'
nigon 'nine'

N*H
nāh 'has not' p. nāhte
nēah adj. 'near, nearly'
ġenēah/ġenōh adj. 'enough'
nēhst adj. 'nearest; latest (of time)'
nīehsta m. 'neighbour'
æt nēhstan 'eventually, in due course'
nāhte p. 'had not'
nāuht, nāht adv. 'not at all; nothing'
niht/neaht F. 'night, darkness'
ġenyht FN 'abundance'

ġenihtsum adj. 'plentiful'
genihtsum-að 'suffices, abounds'
niht-waco F. 'night-watches'
nāhwǣr adv. 'nowhere, no way"

N*L
nēol = neowol 'precipitous,
    headfirst'
nele/nyle, nellað 'does not wish (to)'
    p. nolde
nēalǣċeð/nēalǣhð 'approaches,
    comes close' p. nēalǣhte
nēalîċe adv. 'nearly'
nalæs, nealles adv. 'not at all'

N*M
nam p. 'took'
fornam p. 'destroyed'
nama m. 'name'
nim-ð 'takes, obtains' p. nam/nōm,
    nāmon pp. ġenumen
nemn-an 'to name, call' p. nemde
    pp. ġenemnod
nemne conj. 'unless'
nymðe conj. 'except, unless'

N*N
nān nǣnne etc. pron/adj 'none,
    no one'
nēan adv. '(from) nearby'
nōn 'mid-afternoon; church service
    of nones'
nunne f. 'nun'
nǣniġ adj./pron. 'no one, none'
nānuht adv./pron. 'nothing, not at all'
nānwuht = nānuht

N*P
nîpan 'to darken' p. nāp
nîpende 'darkening'
ġenip N. 'darkness, obscurity'

N*R
nǣre pl. nǣron 'was not, were not'
ner-eð 'saves' p. nerede
nēar adj. 'nearer'
nearu adj. 'oppressive, narrow';
    subst.'danger, difficulty'
    pl. nearwe
nerġend M. 'saviour, Christ'
norð, norðerne adj. 'northern'
norðan adv. 'from the north'
Norð(an)hymbre Mpl. 'Northumbria,
    Northumbrians'
nearwe adv. 'closely, tightly' (= nearu)
nearw-ian 'to confine'
fornearw-ian 'to become unproductive'
neorxna-wang M. 'Paradise'

N*S
næs 'was not' pl. nǣron
næss M. 'headland, cliff'
nese adv. 'no'
nēos-að II 'seeks out, attacks'
nosu F. 'nose'
nāst 'knows not'
nest N. 'nest'
nyste p. 'did not know'
nos-þyrl N. 'nostril'

N*T
nāt 'does not know, is ignorant of'
    pl. nyton
nett N. 'net'
nēat N. 'cattle'
neot-eð/notað 'uses, enjoys' +gen.
nytt adj. 'useful';
    subst. 'use; function'
nyt-an 'not to know'
nāt-hwā adj./pron. 'some one'
nāt-hwilċ adj./pron. 'some sort or
    other'
nȳten N. 'animal'
nytenness F. 'ignorance'
nyttnes F. 'usefulness'

nytente 'shining'

nāteshwōn/nātōþæshwōn adv. 'by no
    means, not at all'

nyt-wyrðe adj. 'notable'

N*TH

ġenēð-eð 'risks, ventures on' p. nēðde

nîð   M. 'violence, hatred'

niðð-as Mpl. 'men'

nōð   F. 'daring; plunder'

ġenîðla m. 'foe'

nȳðemest adj. 'lowest'

neoðan adv. '(from) below, beneath'

nāðer   'neither'

niðer   adv. 'below, downwards'

N*W

nîwe   adj. 'new, fresh'

nāwiht = nāht 'nothing, not at all'

neowol adj. 'precipitous'

niwelnyss F. 'chasm'

nîwan   adv. 'recently'

nāwār adv. 'nowhere'

nēawest F. 'neighbourhood'

N*X

nȳxtan = nîehstan 'nearest, last'

P*C

(be)pǣċ-eð 'seduces, perverts'

piċ   N. 'pitch'

pîċ   M. 'point, pick'

P*D

-pād   'coat, outer covering'

P*L

pæll   M. 'purple cloak'

pîl   M. 'spike, dart'

pyle   'pillow'

palm(a) 'palm-tree'

PL*

plega   m. 'quick movement; activity,
    celebration'

pleġeð 'sports, plays' p. plegode

pleo(h) N. 'peril, danger' gen. plēos

plantian II 'to plant out'

P*N

pîn-að 'tortures'

pun-ode p. 'pounded'

pund   N. 'a pound (weight/money)'

pîn-bēam M. 'pine-tree'

pînn-hnutu F. 'pine-cone'

pening M. 'penny, coin'

P*P

pāpa   m. 'Pope'

pîpdrēam M. 'organ music'

P*R

(for)pǣre subj. 'pervert, destroy'

pearruc M. 'park, enclosed land'

pardus pl. 'leopards'

purpure f. 'purple (cloth)'

port   MN 'port, harbour-town'

PR*

prica   m. 'point, spot; small area or
    time'

pric-að I 'pricks, stings'

prass   M. 'pomp'

prēost M. 'priest'

prȳto   F. 'pride, arrogance'

prēowt-hwîl F. 'blink of an eyelid'

P*S

pistol M. 'letter; epistle'

postol M. 'apostle'

P*T

pytt   M. 'pit, hole'

P*TH

pæð	M. 'path' *pl.* paðas	
peðð-eð	I 'treads, walks'	

R*

rā m. 'roebuck'

R*C

racu F. 'narration, speech'
rǣċan 'to reach out, offer' *p.* rǣhte
ġerǣċan 'to reach, seize, obtain, control'
rēċ M. 'smoke'
ġereċ N. 'rule, government; directive; an uproar'
reċeð 'brings, proffers'
reccan, recceð 'to relate; decide; stretch, extend; care about' *p.* reahte
rēoceð 'smokes, steams'
rîċe N. 'power; kingdom'; adj: 'strong, powerful, rich'
reċed NM 'hall'
ġereċednis F. 'narrative'
reċlîċe adv. 'orderly, straightforwardly, directly'
ġereċlîċe adv. 'in a straight or orderly way'
rēċelēas adj. 'reckless, careless'
rēċels M. 'incense'
reċene adv. 'promptly'
reccend M. 'ruler'
racente f. 'chain'
rîcsað 'rules, reigns' *p.* rîcsode

R*D

rād *p.* 'rode' (rîdan)
rād F. 'riding, journey; raid'
ġerād N. 'assesment, discernment; condition'; adj. 'adapted, special'
rǣd M. 'advice; wisdom; benefit'
rǣd-eð 'reads'
ġerǣ-eð 'advises, designs, arranges'
ġerǣdu N*pl.* 'trappings'

ġerǣde adj. 'prepared'
(ā)rēde *p.* 'he read'
rēad adj. 'red, orange'
rîd-eð 'rides' *p.* rād, ridon
rōd F. 'cross, rood'
rǣdbora m. 'counsellor'
rǣdliċ adj. 'advisable, sensible'
rǣdels 'riddle'
rǣdend M. 'controller, director'
rîdend M. 'rider'
rǣding F. 'a reading; thinking over'
rodor M. 'sky, firmament' *gen.* rodres
radost = hraðost 'speediest'

R*F

rēaf N. 'plunder'; 'clothing'
(be)rēaf-að 'robs, plunders' *p.* berēafode
ġerēfa m. 'reeve, official, sheriff'
rōf adj. 'strong, heroic'
rŷfe adj. 'rife'
rēafere M. 'thief'

R*G

regol M. '(monastic) regulation'
reġn/rēn M. 'rain'
ġereġnad adj. 'decorated'

R*H

rūh adj. 'rough, shaggy' *gen.* rūwes
ġerǣhte *p.* 'reached' (rǣċan)
rehte *p.* 'cared about' (reccan/rēcan)
reht = recceð 'decides, rules'
reahte/rehte *p.* 'stretched; narrated, told' (reccan)
riht adj. 'right, correct etc'; subst. N. 'right, justice, truth'
riht– 'proper, lawful, orthodox'
rihte adv. 'truly, straight etc'
riht-eð I 'puts right; governs'
rihtend M. 'director, ruler'
rihtwîs adj. 'righteous, just, pious'

R*M

ramm	M. 'a ram'
ġerîm	N. 'number, reckoning, count'
(ā)rîm-an	I 'reckon up'
rima	m. 'rim, coast'
Rōm	F. 'Rome'
rūm	adj. 'spacious, generous'
ġerūme	adv. 'widely, amply'
rȳm-an	'to expand, clear, open up' p. rȳmde
rūmheort	adj. 'generous'
Rōmane	pl. 'Romans'

R*N

rān	obl. of rā 'roebuck'
rēn	M. 'rain'
ġerēne	N. 'ornament'
ren-	'hall-'
rîn-eð	'it rains'
rin-eð	'ran' p. ran
rūn	F. 'secret; private talk; a rune'
rȳn	'to growl, roar'
ġerȳne	N. 'mystery'
ryne/rene	MN 'course, orbit, movement'
ranc	adj. 'proud, noble, bold'
rinc	M. 'warrior, man'
rūncofa	m. 'bosom, heart'
rand	M. 'round shield'
ġerēnod	pp. 'arranged, set'
rind(e)	F. 'bark (of tree)'
rēoniġ	adj. 'gloomy'
rūnwita	m. 'wise man, adviser'

R*P

rîp	N. 'harvest'
rîpe	adj. 'ripe'
rîp-að	'ripens' (rîpian)
rîp-eð	'reaps' (rîpan)
rȳp-eð	'robs, plunders' p. rȳpte
repsung	F. 'evening'

R*R

rǽr-eð	'rears, raises' p. rǽrde
reord	FN 'voice'; 'food'
reord-að	'speaks'
reord-berend	M. 'voice-bearer, man'

R*S

rǽs	M. '(on)rush'
rǽs-an	'to rush at, attack' p. rǽsde
rîs-eð/rîst	'rises up; suits, fits' p. (ā)rās
rōse	f. 'rose'
rysel	M. 'lard; resin'
ġerisenliċ	adj. 'suitable, decent'
rāsettan	'to rage (i.e. fire)'
rest	F. 'sleep, rest; bed'
rest-eð	'rests, remains' p. reste
rustiġ	adj. 'rusty'
rǽswa	m. 'leader, director, king'

R*T

rǽt	= rǽdeð 'reads'
rēot-að	pl. 'they weep'
rît	= rîdeð 'rides'
rōt	adj. 'cheerful'
rōtlîċe	adv. 'happily'
rōtnes	F. 'gladness'
rēotiġ	adj. 'tearful'

R*TH

raþe	adv. 'speedily' (hraðe)
rēðe	adj. 'cruel, terrible'
rîð	M. 'runlet'
ryðða	m. 'mastiff'
rēðgodon	ppl. 'raged'
rēðemōd	adj. 'cruel, savage'
rēðen	adj. 'wild'

R*W

rēow	adj. 'rough, fierce' (=hrēoh)
rūwes	gen. of rūh 'rough'
rēwet	N. 'rowing; a boat'
rōwan	'to row, propel'

S*

sǣ	'sea' *gen.* sǣ/sǣs
se	'the, that'
sē	'who, which'
sîe/sî/sȳ	*subj.* 'be!; may be'
sîo	'the; which'

S*B

sibb	F. 'concord, friendship'
ġesibb	adj. 'related'
ġesibsum	adj. 'peace-loving'

S*C

sacu	F. 'struggle, conflict, dispute'; 'right to hold a court' *obl.* sæcce
sac-eð	'struggles with, accuses'
sēċ-þ	'seeks' *p.* sōhte
sēoc	adj. 'sick, ill'
socc	M. 'a sock'
sæcoccas	*pl.* 'cockles'
secg	M. 'people'; 'sword'; 'reed' *pl.* secgas
secgan	'to speak, say' *p.* sæġde
sācerd	M. 'priest'

SC*

scō	'shoe' *pl.* scōn/ġescȳ
scua	m. 'shadow, shade'
sceac-eð	'moves, departed' *p.* scēoc *pp.* scacen
scucca	m. 'evil spirit'
ġescēad	N. 'understanding, meaning'
ġescēad-eð	'divides; decides' *p.* ġescēd
scēad-eð	'scatters, spills'
sceadu	F. 'shadow, shade' *pl.* sceadwe
ġescōd	*p.* 'he injured, hurt' +*dat.*
ġescēadliċ	adj. 'reasonable, sensible'
ġescēadlîċe	adv. 'wisely, properly'
ġescēadwîs	adj. 'prudent, clever'
sceadwe	*pl.* 'shadows'

scūf-eð/scȳfð	'pushes, shoves' *p.* scēaf, scufon *pp.* ġescofen
sceaft	M. 'shaft'
-sceaft	suffix 'state of, condition'
ġesceaft	FMN 'created being, creature; creation'
sceal	'must, has to; should, would' *pl.* sculon *p.* sceolde
sciell	F. 'shell'
scōl	F. 'school'
scolu	F. 'troop, band'
scealc	M. 'man; servant, member of a team'
sceolde	*p.* 'had to, should' (sceal)
scield	M. 'shield; protection'
scyld	FM. 'offence, guilt, sin'
scyldiġ	adj. 'guilty, sinful'
sculdra	*pl.* 'shoulders'
scealfran	*pl.* 'diving birds'
scilling	M. 'shilling'
scîma	m. 'ray of light'
scam-að	II 'it shames'
scamol	M. 'stool'
scamliċ	adj. 'shameful'
scîene	adj. 'beautiful, radiant'
scîn-eð	'shines' *p.* scān
scînende	'shining'
scinn(a)	Nm. 'spectre, illusion; demon'
scinnlāc	N. 'sorcery'
scanca	m. 'shin'
scenċeð	'pours out (a drink)'
scand	F. 'disgrace, scandal'
scendeð	'shames, blames'
scēap	N. 'sheep' *pl.* scēap
ġesceap	N. 'creature; creation, condition'
scip	N. 'ship'
sciepp-eð	'creates, forms' *p.* scēop *pp.* ġesceapen
scōp/(ġe)scēop	*p.* 'created'
scop	M. 'poet, bard'
scipen	N. 'animal shed'
scip-here	M. 'naval force'
scyppend	M. 'creator, i.e. God'

46

ġesceapennys   F. 'formation'
scēar   N. 'plough-share'
scîr   F. 'authority, shire';
   adj. gleaming, clear'
scier-eð   'cuts' *pp.* ġescoren
scūr   M. 'shower, storm'
ġescærp   *p.* 'cut'
scearp   adj. 'sharp, shrewd etc'
scierp-eð   'decks out'; 'sharpens'
   pp. ġescerped
sceorp   N. 'garb, gear'
sceort   adj. 'short'
scrid   N. 'vehicle' *pl.* screodu
scrūd   N. 'clothing, garb'
scrȳdan   I 'to clothe'
scrinċeð   'shrinks, shrivels'
scrîðeð   'moves, glides'
scræf   N. 'cavern, den' *pl.* scrafu
scrîf-eð   'imposes, ordains; shrives'
   p. ġescrāf
scrîn   N. 'chest, shrine'
tō-scēat   *pp.* 'dispersed'
scēat-as   'areas, corner, region'
sceatt   M. 'coin, money'
scēote   f. 'trout'
scēoteð/scȳt   'shoots; rushes'
   p. scēat, scuton
sceot, scyte   N. 'a shooting'
Scottas   pl. 'the Scots; Ireland'
scytta   m. 'archer'
scēotend   M. 'archer'
scēað   'scatters, spills' (= scēadeð)
sceðð-eð   +*dat.* 'injures, hurts'
sceaða/scaða   m. 'harmful or dangerous
   person; enemy'
sceaððiġ   adj. 'dangerous'
scēawað   'gazes, scans' *p.* scēawedon
(fore)scēowað   'pre-ordains'

S*D
sǣd   N. 'seed'
sǣde   *p.* 'said, spoke'
sæd   +*gen.* adj. 'full of, weary of'
sîd   adj. 'wide, ample'
sîde   adv. 'extensively'
sidu/siodu   N*pl.* 'custom, habit' *gen.* sida
sydefull   adj. 'virtuous'
soden   *pp.* 'boiled, cooked'

S*F
sefa   m. 'mind, heart'
seof-að   II 'sighs'
seofon   'seven'
seofontiġ   'seventy'
sȳfre   adj. 'chaste, abstemious'
sēfte/sōfte   adj. 'soft, pleasing, comfy'
seofoða   adj. 'seventh'

S*G
sǣg   *p.* 'sank'
saga   'say!'; subst. 'story'
sîġ-eð   'sinks, goes down'
siġe   M. 'victory; setting, sinking
siġe-   'victorious-'
sǣġde   *p.* 'said, spoke' *pp.* ġesǣġd
seġl   MN. 'sail'
seġlode   *p.* 'sailed'
siġel   'the sun'
siglu   N.*pl.* 'necklaces, jewelry'
sǣġl-rād   M. 'sail-road, sea'
sǣgon/sēgon ppl. 'they saw' = sāwon
seġn   MN. 'sign, banner'
senian   II 'to make the sign of the cross'
sigor   M. 'victory'

S*H
sāh   *p.* 'sank'
seah   *p.* 'saw' (sēon)
seoh   'look!'
seht   MF. 'agreement, settlement'
siehst, siehð   'you, he sees' (sēon)
sōhte   *p.* 'sought'

ġesōhte   p. 'sought out'
sîhŏ   'sinks' (sîgan)
ġesihŏ   F. 'sight'

S*L

sāl   MF. 'rope'
salu, salwiġ–   'dusky, grimy'
sāul   F. 'soul'
sǣl   MF. 'time, occasion'
ġesǣl-eŏ   'happens; binds, ties up'
sēl   adj. 'excellent' cf. sēlra, sēlla
sele   M. 'hall, house'
sel-eŏ   'gives, supplies' p. sealde
sēol-   see seolh 'seal'
sol   N. 'mud'
sūl/sulh   N. 'a plough'
sȳl   F. 'column, pillar'
selliċ   = seldliċ 'rare, strange'
seolc   M. 'silk'
onsǣled   pp. 'untied'
ġesǣlde   p. 'happened'
seld   N. 'hall, palace; seat'
sealde   p. 'gave' pp. ġeseald
seldcūŏ   adj. 'unusual, rare'
seldliċ   adj. 'rare, strange'
seldan   adj. 'seldom' comp. seldnor;
    superl. seldost
self/selfa   pron. '(my)self,
    (your)self, (him)self,
(them)selves etc'
sealf   F. 'ointment'
selfliċ   adj. 'vain'
seolfor   N. 'silver' gen. seolfres
seolfren   adj. 'made of silver'
ġesǣliġ   adj. 'happy, lucky'
seolh   M. 'seal' pl. sēolas
sulh   N. 'plough' gen. sylh/sūles
seolh-bæŏ   N. 'the sea'
sealm   M. 'psalm'
sol-mōnaŏ   M. 'February'
sēlra   adj. 'better'
sēlost   adj. 'best, finest'

sylst   'you give' (sellan)
sealt   N. 'salt'
sylt-an   'to salt'
saltere   M. 'Psalter'
sealtere   M. 'salt-maker'
ġesǣlŏ   F. 'good fortune, happiness'
ġesǣlŏ   'occurs, happens'
salwiġ   obl. of salu 'dusky'

SL*

sleac   adj. 'slack, lax'
slecg   M. 'sledge-hammer'
slîd-eŏ   'slides'
slidor   adj. 'slippery'
slege   M. 'beating, slaughter'
slōg/slōh   'struck, impelled'
    pp. ġeslǣgen
sleh-ŏ   'strikes'
slōh   = slōg
slēan   'to strike, beat, slay'
slǣp   M. 'sleep'
slǣp-eŏ   pl. slāpaŏ 'sleeps' p. slǣpte
slūp-an   'to slip away' pp. slopen
slît-an   'to slit; wound'
    p. slāt, sliton
slîŏe   adj. 'ferocious, dangerous'
slāw   adj. 'slow, lazy'

S*M

sām–   'half-, partly–'
sam   conj. 'whether, or'
sam–   'in union, unison'
(swā) same   'the same, likewise'
sǣum   dat.pl. of sǣ 'sea'
ġesēm-an   I 'to reconcile'
seom-aŏ   II 'tarries, continues'
sum   pron. 'a certain –, some –';
    +gen. 'one of'
sim(b)le, symle   adv. 'continually, ever'
symbel   N. 'feast, festival'
samod   adv. 'together, simultaneously'
sumdǣl   'somewhat'
samn-aŏ   'gathered' pp. ġesomnod

samnung F. 'union, assembly'
samnunga/semninga adv. 'straight away'
sæmra adj. 'worse, inferior'
sæ-maras pl. 'sea-horses, ships'
sēamere M. 'seamster, tailor'
sumor M. 'summer'
samtinges adv. 'at once'
sāmwîs adj. 'dull, not clever'

SM*
smēagan/smēan hē smēað 'think,
    consider' p. smēade
smūgan 'to creep'
smēagung F. 'thought, reflection'
smæl adj. 'small'
smolt adj. 'gentle, mild'
smylte adv. 'mildly'
smaragdus 'emerald'
smirwan 'to annoint'
smēade p. 'he thought'
smēðe adj. 'smooth'
smið M. 'craftsman, blacksmith'

S*N
sæne adj. 'slack, careless'
(ġe)sēon 'to see'
sîn adj. 'his, hers, its'
sin– (pref.) 'continual-'
sîen 'be' (subj. pl.)
sōna adv. 'directly, at once'
sunne f. 'Sun' gen. sunnen
sunu M. 'son; descendant' gen. suna
ġesŷne adj. 'visible, evident'
syn(n) F. 'sin'
sanc = sang 'sang'
senċ-eð 'submerges, wets' p. senċte
sinc N. 'treasure'
sinc-ġyfa m. 'treasure-giver, lord'
sanct M. 'saint'
sand N. 'sand'; F. 'sending, course of
    food'
send-eð/sent 'sends' pp. sended
send-on ppl. 'they sent'

sind/sindon 'are'
sund N. 'swimming; voyage; the sea'
ġesund adj. 'safe, healthy, whole'; sim.
    ansund, ġesundful
sundbūende Mpl. 'humans'
sundor adv. 'apart'
sundor– 'special, private'
(ā)sundrad pp. 'sundered (from)'
synderlic adj. 'special'
syndriġ adj. 'separate, various'
sinniġ adj. 'crinimal'
sang M. 'song, singing'; p. 'he sang'
sing-eð 'sings' p. sang
syng-að 'he sins'
singal adj. 'perpetual, continuous'
Sunnan-dæġ M. 'Sunday'
sænra adj. 'slower, worse'
sinscipe M. 'marriage, living together'
sunstede M. 'equinox'
sent = sendeð 'sends'
sint 'are'
ġesynto F. 'health, welfare, prosperity'
sinoð F. 'synod'
sinewealt adj. 'globular'

SN*
snîċ-eð 'sneaks along'
(be)snædan 'to cut, slash'
snofliġ adj. 'snotty'
snell adj. 'smart, prompt, bold'
snēome adv. 'speedily'
snyrġan 'to hurry'
snotor adj. 'clever, wise'
snyttru F. 'sagacity, wisdom'
snîð-eð 'cuts' p. snāð, snidon
snāw M. 'snow'
snēow-an 'to hurry'
snîw-eð 'it snows'

S*P
sāp(e) 'sap, resin'
sæpiġ adj. 'sappy, green'
sūpeð 'swallows, drinks'

SP*

spæċ	p. 'spoke'
spēd	F. 'success, resources'
spēd-eð	'succeeds, works well; is rich'
spell	N. 'story, homily'
spell-ode	p. 'spoke, narrated'
spill-an	'to spoil, destroy' p. spilde
(ā)spyl-ian	'to wash (oneself)'
spann-eð	'entices, persuades; joins, fastens'
spere	N. 'spear, lance' pl. speoru
spyr-að	'pursues, tracks' p. spyrede
spar-að	'spares, saves'
spearc-ian	II 'to spark'
spearca	m. 'a spark'
spor	N. 'trail, spoor'
spyrte	f. 'basket, whicker trap'
sprǣċ	F. 'speech, language'
spreċ-ð	'speaks' p. spræċ, sprǣcon
spranc	p. 'sprang, burst out, spread'
spring	M. 'spring (of water)'
spring-eð	'springs up, arises' p. sprang
spearwa	m. 'sparrow'
sprēot	M. 'pike, spear'
sprytt-að	pl. 'they sprout up'
spittan	'to spit; to dig in'
spiweð	'spit out, spew up'
spōw-eð	'it benefits, helps someone' p. spēow

S*R

sār	N. 'pain, suffering'; adj. 'sore, painful'
sāre	adv. 'sorely'
(for)sēar-að	II 'withers'
searo	N. 'cunning, art; trick, snare' dat.pl. searwum
searo–	'clever, artistic, ingenious'
syrċe	f. 'coat of mail'
serede	p. 'prepared, readied'
sāriġ	adj. 'sorry, unhappy'
sārg-ode	p. 'caused or felt pain'
sorg/sorh	F. 'sorrow, anxiety'

sorg-ian	'to sorrow, care (for)' p. sorgode
sǣ-rima	m. 'coast'
searw-	see searo
searwum	adv. 'cunningly'
sierw-an	'to devise, entrap; to kit out'

S*S

sūsl	NF 'torment, torture'

S*T

sæt	'sat' pl. sǣton
sett-eð	'sets, places, ordains' pp. ġeset
ġeset	N. 'seat, dwelling'
ġesette	p. 'established, placed'
sit-eð/sitt	'sits, abides'
sot	adj. 'foolish'
setl	N. 'seat, throne, residence'
setlung	F. 'setting'
gesetnes	F. 'ordinance; founding; arrangement, disposition'
Sæternesdæġ	M. 'Saturday'

ST*

stede	M. 'place, site'
stiċe	M. 'sting; stabbing pain'
stiċ-að	II 'stabs'; 'adheres' p. sticode
stōd, stōdon	'stood'
stedefæst	adj. 'steady'
stæf	M. 'stave; letter' pl. statas
stæfgeťeġ	'syllable'
stefn	F. 'voice'
stefna	m. 'duty, turn; stem, tree-trunk, prow'
stiġ	FM 'path, track'
stīġ-eð	'ascends; descends' p. stāg, stigon pp. stiġen
stāh	= stāg 'ascended, descended'
stīh-ð	'climbs' (stīgan)
stiht-eð	'directs, incites' p. stihte
stōl	M. 'chair, throne'
stalu	F. 'theft'
stela	m. 'stalk'

steall M. 'stall; status'
ġestēaled pp. 'extended'
onsteal-de p. 'instituted'
-ġestealla m. '-companion'
stille adj. 'still'
ġestill-an 'to stop, become still'
pp. ġestilled
stȳle N. 'steel'
styll-an 'to put into stalls; to rush, attack'
stealc adj. 'steep'
ġesteald N. 'residence'
stylnes F. 'stillness'
stemm F. 'stem, trunk' (= stefn)
stēam M. 'moisture'
stān M. 'stone'
ġe-stun N. 'din; chaos'
stun-að II 'crashes, roars'
stenċ M. 'odour, fragrance, smell'
stinċ-eð 'smells, gives or receives smell; scatters'
stand-eð/stent 'stands; remains, is' p. stōd
wið-stondan 'to withstand, oppose'
stund F. 'short time; an hour'
stundum adv. 'at intervals'
sting-eð 'stings, stabs' p. stang
stent = standeð 'stands'
stunt adj. 'stupid'
-stapa m. '-walker'
stæpe M. 'pace, step' pl. stapas
stæp-eð 'steps onward, goes' p. stōp
stēap adj. 'lofty, projecting'
stapol M. 'column, post'
stær N. 'history'
star-að II 'stares'
stēor 'steering, discipline'
stēora m. 'steersman'
steorra m. 'star'
stīor-de p. 'steered, directed'
stir 'confusion'
stȳr-eð I 'steers, controls'

styr-ian II 'to move, stir, incite'
pp. ġestyred
styria m. 'sturgeon'
stearc adj. 'rigid, stern'
stēorlēas adj. 'uncontrolled'
storm M. 'storm; violent action'
styrm-eð 'storms, shouts'
stearn M. 'tern'
steort M. 'tail'
stēor-rōþer N. 'rudder'

[STR]
strīċ-eð 'rubs; moves'
strēd-an 'to strew, scatter'
strūd-an 'to rob, plunder'
strugdon ppl. 'scattered, spread'
pp. stræġd
ġestreht pp. 'stretched'
stræl M. 'arrow'
strēam M. 'current, water'
ġestrēon N. 'profit, treasure'
strīn-eð 'acquires; begets'
ppl. strȳndon
strȳnd F. 'descent, stock'
strang adj. 'strong, firm'
strengðu F. 'strength'
strǣt F. 'paved street'
stæð MN 'shore, bank'
pl. staðas/staðu
stīð adj. 'stiff, strong, strict'
staðol M. 'foundation; station'
ġestaðolian II 'to found, establish'
staðolfæst adj. 'fixed'
stōw F. 'spot, site'

S*TH
sēað M. 'pit, hole'
sēoð 'they see' (sēon)
sēoð-eð 'seethes, boils' p. sēað
sīð M. 'occasion, journey, departure'
ġesīð M. 'companion; warrior'
sūð 'south'

sîð-fæt	N. 'journey, expedition'
sōð	N. 'truth, certainty';
	adj. 'true, sure'
sōðfæst	adj. 'honest, righteous'
sōðlîċe	adv. 'truly'
siþþan	adv./conj. 'since, when'
sūþan	adv. 'from the south'
suþerne	adj. 'southern'

S*W

sāw-eð	'sows (seed)' pp. ġesāwen
sēaw	M. 'juice'
sîow-(i)an	'to sew'
suw-að	II 'become silent'
sāwol	F. 'soul' gen. sāwle
ġesewenliċ	adj. 'visible'
sāwon	ppl. 'saw' (sēon)

SW*

swā	adv. 'so, just as';
	conj. 'as, like'
ġeswāc	p. 'ceased, failed'
swæċ	M. 'flavour'
swîċ-eð	'moves, goes; ceases, fails;
	betrays' p. swāc
swica	m. 'betrayer'
swiċdom	M. 'fraud'
swicol	adj. 'deceitful'
swef-eð	'sleeps; puts to sleep, kills'
	p. swæf, swæfon
swefn	N. 'sleep; dream'
sweofot	N. 'slumber'
swift	adj. 'swift'
swēġ	M. 'sound'
swēġ-don	ppl.'roared; made a noise'
swîġe	adj. 'silent';
	subst. 'silence'
swîg-að/swūg-að	'becomes silent'
swōg-an	'to roar, make a noise'
sweġl	N. 'sky, the heavens'
sweġle	adv./adj. 'brilliant, clearly'
swel-eð	'burns, smoulders'
swelċ/swilċ	pron. 'such a one, the same'

swylċe	adv./conj. 'likewise; as if'
swelg-eð	'swallows'
swealg/swealh	pl. swulgon 'swallowed'
swelt-an	'to die, perish' ppl. swulton
swylt	M. 'death'
swalewan	pl. 'swallows (birds)'
sweoloð	M. 'fire, heat'
swim-eð	'floats, swims' p. swom
swān	M. 'swineherd; local youth'
swan	M. 'swan'; –rād 'the sea'
swîn	N. 'wild-boar, pig'
swenċ-eð	'harasses, troubles'
swinċ	N. 'toil, hard work; hardship, problems'
swinċ-eð	'labours; struggles; is in trouble' p. swanc
sweng	M. 'a stroke or blow'
sweng-eð	'rushes, flies'
swing-eð	'whips, flogs' ppl. swungon
swinsade	p. 'sweetly sounded'
swinsung	F. 'melody'
swāp-eð	'sweeps, rushes' ppl. swēopon
swāp-eð	'swept, rushed' p. swēop
swipu	F. 'whip, scourge'
swēor	MF 'pillar'
swēora/swȳra	m. 'neck'
swer-ian	'to swear'
swearċ-eð	'becomes dark' p. swearc
sweord	N 'sword'
sworfen	pp. 'ground up'
swirm-an	'to swarm (of bees)'
sweart	adj. 'black, dark, evil'
swæs	adj. 'intimate, favourite'
swæsendu	N.pl. 'dinner'
sweostor/swuster	F. 'sister'
swāt	M. 'sweat; blood'
swæteð/swæt	'sweats, exudes'
swēte	adj. 'sweet, pleasant'
swutol	adj. 'clear, evident'
sweotole	adv. 'plainly'
swutel-að	'shows, displays' p. sweotolode

swæð N. 'track, footprint'
  pl. swaðu
swaðul 'a flame'
swīþe adv. 'very'
swā-þēah adv. 'however'
swīðliċ adj. 'powerful'
sweðr-að II 'abates, subsides'
swīðor 'more strong(ly), quick(ly); right-hand'
swīðre 'on the right'
swīð-rað II 'is strong, prevails'

S*X
six 'six'
sēax M. 'hip-knife'
Seaxe M*pl.* 'the Saxons'
ġesyxt = ġesihð 'sees'

T*
tō prep. +*dat.* 'to, into, towards, at'
tō adv. 'towards, besides; too, also'
tō– 'to, towards; apart, asunder'
tēo 'I tug; I accuse'
tū 'two'

T*B
tō-blāweð 'blows away, scatters'
tō-breċeð 'breaks to pieces'
tō-brædeð 'broadcasts, disperses'

T*C
tǣċ-ð 'teaches; declares'
tūc-að 'ill-treats'
tōcyme M. 'arrival, advent'
tācn N. 'symbol, sign' *pl.* tācn(u)
tācn-að II 'denotes, signifies'
  p. tācnode
tō-ēacen 'besides, in addition'
tō-cnāweð 'knows, recognises'
tō-ċorfeð 'cuts off, cuts away'

T*D
ġetēde *p.* 'prepared'
tīd F. 'hour; time; season'
tīd-eð 'happens'
tīode *p.* 'ordained'
tȳde *pl.* tȳdon 'instructed'
tō-dǣleð 'divides, distributes'
  pp. tōdǣlde
tōdæġ 'today'
tūdor N. 'offspring, descendant'
tȳdr-eð 'begets, produces'
tȳdre adj. 'weak, frail'
tō-drīfeð 'drives away, scatters'
tȳdreness F. 'frailty'

T*F
tō-flōweð 'flows away'
tōforan +*dat.* 'before' (time/place)
tefrung F. 'circle'

T*G
tīġ-eð 'ties'
tyġe M. 'tugging, leading'
tæġl M. 'tail'
ġetiġen *pp.* 'accused'
ġetogen *pp.* 'restrained'
tugon *ppl.* 'drew, tugged'
tōgædre adv. 'together'
tiġel(e) Ff. 'earthenware item'
tōġēanes adv. 'towards, against, in return'
tiger M. 'tiger' *pl.* tigras

T*H
tēah *p.* 'tugged'; 'accused'
ġetēah *p.* 'drew out'
tāh *p.* 'accused'
teohh-ian II 'to determine, assess, ordain'
tiohhung F. 'disposition, arrangement'
tō-hopa m. 'hope'
tȳhsð 'you draw, pull'
tǣhte, tēhte *p.* 'taught, demonstrated'

tîhteð/tîhð 'accuses'
tîhð 'draws, pulls'
tyht M. 'instruction'
tyht-eð I 'pulls; persuades; teaches'

T*L
tal-að 'counts, reckons'
tæl F. 'blame, reproach'
ġetæl-eð 'blames, reproaches'
ġetæl/ġetel N. 'number, count, tally'
    pl. ġetalu
tela/teola adv. 'well, correctly'
tel-eð 'estimates, tells, esteems'
    p. ġeteald
til-að II 'intends, strives'
till N. 'position, station'
til adj. 'good, excellent'
tōl N. 'tool'
toll MN 'levy'
ġeteld N. 'tent'
telga m. 'branch'
telg M. 'dye'
tō-lȳseð 'loosens, dissolves'
tealt adj. 'unsteady, moving,
    tipping'
tilð F. 'farm-work; crop'

T*M
tam adj. 'tame'
tama m. 'tameness'
tēam M. 'lineage, offspring';
    'jurisdiction over guarantees'
tem-eð 'tames' *pp.* ġetemed
tîma m. 'time, period'
tîem-eð I 'begets, produces'
ġetimbru F. 'timbers, a building'
timbredon *ppl.* 'built'
tōmiddes +*dat.* 'in the middle of'
templ N. 'temple'
Temes(e) Ff. 'the Thames'

T*N
tān M. 'twig, shoot, stripe'
tēon 'to tug, pull; to accuse; to
    arrange, produce'
tēona m. 'pain, injury'
tēon– 'hurtful-'
tîen/tȳn 'ten'
tin N. 'tin'
tūn M. 'enclosure, garden, town'
tȳn-eð 'irritates, insults'
tuneċe f. 'tunic, coat'
be-tȳned *pp.* 'enclosed, shut'
ġetenge 'near to'
ġeteng-de *p.* 'closed with'
tunge f. 'tongue'
tungol NM 'star, planet'
    gen. tungles
tintreġ N. 'torture'

T*P
tapor M. 'candle'
tæppere M. 'tavern-keeper'

T*R
ter-eð 'rends, tears' *p.* tær, tæron
tēar M. 'drop, tear'
(ā)tēorian, tēorað 'tire, cease'
    pp. ġetēorud
tîr M. 'fame, glory'
tor(r) M. 'tower; crag'
tor-að 'towers up'
tîr-ēadiġ(-fæst) adj. 'glorious, famous'
turf F. 'turf, ground' *obl.* tyrf-
torfod *pp.* 'stoned'
torht adj. 'glorious, bright'
torn N. 'anger; grief'
turn-að 'turns'
ymbtyrnd *pp.* 'turned round'
turtur/turtla Mm. 'turtle-dove'

TR*
trîo   = trēow 'trees'
tred-eð/tritt   'treads (on)' *p.* treddode
ātrefed   *pp.* 'drawn, depicted'
traht   M. 'text; commentary'
trum   adj. 'sound, fit'
untrum   adj. 'ill, invalid'
trym-að   'encourages, sets in order'
      p. trymede
trumliċ   adj. 'firm, durable'
trumnes   F. 'health, reliability'
trendel   N. 'orb'
træppe   f. 'a trap'
tritt   'treads' (tredan)
trēow   N. 'tree; timber'
trēow   F. 'trust, faith, promise'
ġetrîewe   adj. 'true, honest, loyal'
trūwað/trēoweð 'trusts'; *p.* trūwode

T*S
ġetǣse   N. 'usefulness';
      adj. 'convenient, helpful'
tōscēot-eð   'shoots apart'
tōslît-eð   'tears apart' *p.* tōslāt
tōsomne   adv. 'together'

T*T
tōtwǣm-eð   'differentiates; breaks up'

T*TH
tîð   F. 'permission'; or verb
      (tēon) 'pulls; accuses;
      arranges'
tōð   M. 'tooth' *pl.* tēð
tîð-að   II 'grants'
tēoð   'they drag; they accuse'
tēoða   adj. 'tenth'

T*W
tāw-að   'readies; harries'
Tîw   'God of war'
tuwa   adv. 'twice'
tōweard   adj. 'oncoming,
      approaching';
      prep/adv. 'towards'
tō-weorpan   'to demolish' *p.* tōwearp
Tîwesdæġ   'Tuesday'

TW*
twā   'two'
twēode   *p.* 'was doubtful, uncertain'
ġetwǣfde   *p.* 'divided'
twifeald   adj. 'double'
twig   N. 'twig'
twēġen   M. (twā F.; tū N.) 'two'
      gen. twēġea *dat.* twǣm
twēoliċ   adj. 'doubtful'
twelf   'twelve'
twǣm   *dat.* 'to two'
twǣman   I 'to divide (into two)'
twēntiġ   'twenty'

T*X
tuxas   M*pl.* 'tusks'

TH*
þā   *nom. acc. pl.* 'the, those;
      who, which'
þā   adv. 'then'; conj. 'when'
þē   *acc./dat.* 'thee'
þē   'the' (late texts only)
þe   (indecl.) 'which'
þū   'you, thou'
þȳ   'by which, in that'

TH*C
ðaċ-ian   'to thatch'
þæċ   N. 'thatch'
þeċċan, þeċeð   'covers'
þicce   adj. 'thick, dense'
þicgan, þiġeð   'receives, consumes'

þeċele f. 'torch'
þiċnys F. 'thickness, opaqueness'

TH*D
þēod F. 'people, nation; country;
language'
ġeþēod-eð 'joins (with)'
þēode p. 'he flourished'
ġeþēode N. 'speech, language, nation'
þēoden M. 'leader, lord (of a tribe or
nation)'
þoden M. 'whirlwind'
þider adv. 'on that side'
þēodscipe M. 'nation; community'

TH*F
þaf-ian 'to permit, consent to; suffer,
endure' p. ġeþafode
ġeþæf +gen. 'consenting (to)'
þēof M. 'thief'
ðȳflas Mpl. 'bushes, undergrowth'
ġeþafung F. 'consent'
geþofta m. 'comrade, fellow crew-
member'

TH*G
þiġeð 'receives, consumes p. þǣg,
þǣgon pp. ġeþiġen
þug-on ppl.'they flourished'
þeġn M. 'thane, official; attendant'
þeġn-að 'serves' p. þeġnode
þeġnung F. 'service'

TH*H
þēoh N. 'thigh'
þeahte p. 'covered'
geþeaht N. 'divising'
ġeþōhte p. 'he thought' (ðencan)
geþōht M. 'thinking, thought'
þūhte p. 'it seemed' (ðyncan)
þīhtiġ adj. 'sturdy'
ġeþeahtere M. 'counsellor'

TH*L
þol-að 'suffers, endures, survives'
p. þolode
ġeþyldiġ adj. 'patient'
þyling F. 'planking'
ġeþyld F. 'patience'

TH*M
þām, þǣm dat.pl. 'to the, to those, to
whom'

TH*N
þēn = þeġn 'official, thane;
attendant'
þēon 'to prosper, do well'
þen-eð 'stretches, extends'
þīn 'your, thine'
þone acc. M. sg. 'the, that'
þon instr. MN. sg. '(by) the, that'
þonne adv. 'then'; conj. 'when; than'
þun-að 'thunders, roars'
þynne adj. 'thin'
þanc-að 'thanks'
ġeþonc 'favourable thought,
gratitude; thought, mind'
þenċeð/þinċeð 'thinks (of)' p. þōhte
þynċ-eð 'it seems' p. þūhte
þancful/þoncol adj. 'thoughtful,
sensible'
þindeð 'swells up'
þing N. 'thing, matter, cause'
þing-ian 'to intercede; plan';
pp. ġeþingod 'settled'
þengel M. 'prince, ruler'
ġeþungen pp. 'full-grown, well-
grown'
þanon adv. 'from there, thence'
þīnen F. 'handmaiden'
þēnung F. 'service'
þunor M. 'thunder' gen. þunres

TH*R

þǣr	adv. 'there'; conj. 'where'
þǣre	gen. dat. F. sg. 'of, to, the, that'
þāra	gen. pl. 'of the, those'
þearf	F. 'need, necessity'
þearfa	m. 'poor man'
þearf	'needs (to), has to'
	p. þorfte pl. þurfon
þurh	prep. 'through, by means of'; adv. 'through, all over'
þǣr-rihte	adv. 'directly, instantly'
þearl	adj. 'strong, strict'
þearle	adv. 'harshly, very'
þyrel	N. 'hole'
þǣr-an	'therein, thereof'
þǣr-inne	adv. 'therein'
þorn	M. 'thorn (tree)'
ġeþuren	pp. 'compressed'
ðerscan	'to thresh'
þerscwold	M. 'threshold'
þyrsteð	'thirsts'
þǣr-tō	adv. 'thereto'

THR*

þrēa	Fm. 'threat, attack'
þrî, þrēo	'three'
þri–	'three-'
ġeþrǣċ	N. 'mob; violence'
þracu	F. 'violence, onrush'
	gen. þrǣċe
þryġ-eð	'tramples on'
þrǣd	M. 'thread'
þrēade	p. 'afflicted'
þridda	adj. 'third'
þrāg	F. 'period of time, occasion'
þrǣġ-eð	'runs'
þrēaġ-eð	'threatens; punishes'
	pp. ġeþrēad
þroht	M. 'heavy work, trouble'
þrǣl	M. 'serf, slave'
þrim	dat. 'to three'
þrymm	M. 'power, glory; crowd'

þrēa-nŷd	F. 'strict compulsion'
þring-eð	'presses on, crowds, cramps'
	pp. ġeþrungen
ġeþrang	N. 'throng, crowd, tumult'
þrinis	F. 'the Trinity'
þrǣst-eð	'twists, torments'
	pp. ġeþrǣsted
þrîst	adj. 'daring, adventurous'
þrostle	f. 'thrush'
þrēat	M. 'a crowd; coercion'
þrotu	F. 'throat'
þrēatedon	'forced, rebuked, threatened' pp. ġeþrēatod
þrîtiġ	'thirty'
þrŷð	F. 'might. majesty'; adj. 'bold, mighty'
þrŷðliċ	adj. 'valiant'
þrōw-ian	'to suffer' p. þrōwode
þrōwung	F. 'suffering, martyrdom'

TH*S

þās	'these'
þæs	gen. MN sg. 'of the, that'
þæs	adv. 'after; to that (degree)'
þes	'this'
þēos	'this'
þus	adv. 'thus'
þŷs	instr. MN sg. 'by this'
þæs-liċ	adj. 'suitable'
þūsend	'a thousand'
þēostru	F. 'shadows, darkness'
þeostr-að	II 'becomes dark'
þeostriġ	adj. 'dark'

TH*T

þæt	'the, that'; conj. '(so) that'
þætte	conj. 'so that'
þēotan, hē þŷt	'to roar, howl'

TH*TH

þŷð	'presses, pushes; forces'
þōþer	M. 'ball'

TH*W

þāw-að 'thaws'
þēaw M. 'habit, custom, manners'
þēow MF. 'servant, slave'
þēow-eð I 'presses, forces' *p.* ðēwde
þēow-að II 'serves; enslaves'
þēaw-fæst adj. 'virtuous'
þȳwan I 'to press, push'

THW*

þwyhð 'washes'
þwēal N. 'washing'
þwang M. 'a thong'
geþwǣre adj. 'harmonious, co-operative'
þweorh adj. 'bent; adverse' *gen.* þwēores
geþwǣrliċ adj. 'congruous, in harmony'
geþwǣrlǣċð 'agrees; suits'
þwēorliċ adj. 'contrary, awkward'
þwēor-tēme adj. 'perverse, contrary'

TH*X

þūxað 'darkens'

W*

wā/wēa M. 'woe, misery'; wā! 'alas!'
wē 'we'
wō = wōh adj. 'crooked, perverse'

W*B

web N. 'weaving, tapestry'

W*C

wāc adj. 'weak, feeble'
wāc-eð 'becomes weak'
wac-ian, wac-eð II 'awakes, is born'
weċ-eð 'rouses, wakes s.one up'
wīc N. 'village; trading-post'
wīc-að 'dwells'
wicca m. 'wizard'
wucu F. 'week' *gen.pl.* wucena

wecg M. 'lump (of metal)'
wecg-að 'they disturb, move about'
wicg N. 'horse'
wāc-liċ adj. 'pathetic'
wacol adj. 'wakeful, alert'
wæċn-eð 'comes into being'
wæccende/waċiende 'watchful'
wīcing M. 'Viking'

W*D

wād N. 'woad'
wadu N*pl.* 'waters, sea'
wǣd F. 'dress, clothing; sail'
wæd-eð 'moves' *pl.* wadað *p.* wōd(on) *pp.* ġewaden
wēd-eð I 'rages, goes berserk' *ppl.* wēddon
wedd N. 'pledge, agreement'
wēod N. 'herb; weed'
wōd adj. 'mad'
ġewōd *p.* 'went; pervaded'
wīde adv. 'widely'
wudu FM 'wood, timber; tree; a wood' *gen.* wuda, wudes
wǣdl F. 'poverty'
wǣdla m. 'a poor person'
Wōdenesdæġ 'Wednesday'
weder N. 'weather'; 'storm'
wīdur adj. 'wider'

W*F

wāf-að 'is amazed; admires'
(be)wǣfed *pp.* 'enwrapped'
wēofod N. 'altar'
wīf N. 'woman'
wīf-cȳð 'female company'
wǣfels MN 'a cloak'
wīf-mann M. 'woman'
wāfung F. 'display, spectacle'
wǣfre adj. 'wavering, errant'
wǣfersîn F. 'spectacle, display'

58

W*G

wāg	M. 'wall'
wag-edon	ppl. 'wagged, swayed'
wǣġe	N. 'cup'
wǣġ	M. 'wave; the sea'
wǣġ-	'wavy-patterned-'
wǣġ-eð	'troubles, upsets'
	pp. ġewēġed
weġ	M. 'way, path, route'
	pl. wegas
weġ-eð	'carries, supports'
wîġ	N. 'conflict, battle'
wîġ–	'war-'
wiga	m. 'fighter'
wiġ-bed	M. 'altar'
wiġl-ian	'to make magic'
wiġlung	f. 'sorcery'
wæġn	M. 'waggon, vehicle'
wîġend	M. 'warrior'

W*H

wāh = wāg	'wall'
wōh	adj. 'bent, kinked, bad'
wî-haga	m. 'war-hedge, shield-wall'
wōh-hǣmed	N. 'adultery'
wiht, wuht	FN 'being, creature';
	adv. 'at all'

W*L

wālā!/wālāwā!	'alas!, woe!'
wæl	N. 'slaughter, violent death'
	pl. walu
wel	adv. 'well, easily'
wel–	'almost, nearly'; 'well, good'
Wēalas	Mpl. 'the Welsh; Wales'
weall	M. 'wall, rampart'
weall-eð	'seethes, rages, boils'
	p. wēoll pp. ġeweallen
wile	'he wishes'
wil–	'willing, friendly'
willa	m. 'will, desire'; sim. ġewill
wiell(a)	Mm 'spring, fountain';
	pref. wyll(e)–

wōl	'plague'
wull	F. 'wool'
wealc-an	'to roll' p. weolc
	pp. ġewealcen
weolc	M. 'whelk'
wolcn	N. 'cloud; sky'
wæl-cyriġe	f. 'witch'
weald	M. 'forest'
ġeweald	N. 'power, authority'
wilde	adj. 'wild'
weald-eð	'rules, controls' +gen.
wolde	p. 'he wished, would'
ġeweald-leðer	N. 'rein'
wealdend	M. 'ruler, esp. God'
wuldor	N. 'glory'
weliġ	adj. 'rich, wealthy'
welig-að	'prospers'
wæl-hrēow	adj. 'savage, bloodthirsty
wealh-stod	M. 'translator'
wel-hwā	'anyone'
wel-hwǣr	'nearly everywhere'
wealh	M. 'foreigner, slave,
	Welshman' gen. weales
wylm/wielm	M. 'surge'
w(e)allende	'raging, boiling'
wiln-að	'wishes, longs (for)'
	p. wilnode
wilnung	F. 'desire, longing'
weleras	Mpl. 'lips'
wæl-stōw	F. 'battlefield'
welt/wilt	'he rules' +gen.
wilt	'you wish'
wielt	'rules, governs'
wealw-að	'rolls; shrivels up'

WL*

wlanc	adj. 'splendid, proud'
wlætta	m. 'loathing'
wlît-an	'to look upon' p. wlāt
wlite	M. 'beauty'
wlitiġ	adj. 'beautiful'
wlætta	m. 'loathing, nausea'
wlite-sēon	F. 'spectacle'

W*M

wamm	M. 'stain; corruption'
wem-eð	'defiles, smears'
wōma	m. 'noise, alarm'
wamb	F. 'belly'

W*N

wǣn	= wæġn 'cart'
wana	m. 'lack'
wan-að	'lessens, declines'
	pp. ġewaned
wēn	FM 'hope, expectation';
	also wēna m.
wēn-eð	'hopes, imagines, expects'
	p. wēnde
wen-að	'accustoms, trains'
	p. ġewenede
wîn	N. 'wine'
wine	M. 'friend'
win-eð	'struggles, competes'
ġewinn-an	'to beat, win'
	pp. ġewunnen
ġewinn	N. 'toil, hardship; conflict'
won/wan	adj. 'colourless, lustreless, dark; feeble'
ġewuna	m. 'custom'
wun-að	'dwells, inhabits; remains'
	p. wunode
wyn	F. 'joy'
wand	p. 'twisted, curled, meandered'
bewand	p. 'clasped'
wend-eð	'goes, wends; changes'
āwend-eð	'turns, alters, translates'
wind	M. 'wind'
wind-eð	'curls, twists; flies, leaps'
	p. wand
wund	F. 'wound'
wunode	p. 'dwelled'
wunden	adj. 'wound up, twisted'
āwunden	pp. 'woven, twisted'
wundon	ppl. 'wound' (wendan)

wanung	F. 'diminution, waning'
wîn-ġeard	M. 'vineyard; ?vine'
Wendel-sǣ	'the Mediterranean'
wynlēas	adj. 'joyless'
wandr-að	'wanders, flies about'
wundor	N. 'a marvel'
wundr-að	'marvels at' p. wundrode
wundrum	adv. 'marvellously'
wang/wong	M. 'a plain'
wange	n. 'jaw, cheek'
wan-hāl	adj. 'unwell'
wynnum	adv. 'joyfully';
	or dat. pl. of wyn
ġewunelic	adj. 'customary, usual'
wynsum	adj. 'pleasant, charming'
winstre	f. 'left-hand'; adj. 'left'
went	'goes' (wendan)
winter	N. 'winter; years'
winde-winċle	f. '(peri)winkle'

W*P

wǣpn	N. 'weapon'
wēp-eð	'weeps' p. wēop
wōp	M. 'crying, lamentation'
wǣpned	adj. 'armed'

W*R

wār	N. 'seaweed'
war-að	'is wary; guards'
-ware, -waran	pl. 'inhabitants, citizens (of)'
wǣr	F. 'good faith; treaty'
wǣr	adj. 'wary, cautious'
wer	M. 'man'
wer	M. 'weir; trap for fish'
wer-að	'guards, defends' p. werode
wærc	N. 'pain, suffering'
weorc	N. 'work, labour, suffering, pain'
ġeweorc	N. 'work, built structure'
wyrċð	'works, makes, does'
weard	M. 'keeper, guardian'

werod   N. 'crowd; an army subdivision'
word   N. 'word, speech, saying'
wurd-on   *ppl.* 'became, were' *pp.* ġeworden
wyrd   F. 'event, outcome; fate, history'
forwyrd   F. 'damnation'
wyrd-an   'to spoil, damage, injure' *pp.* werded/āwyrded
wariġan   'to beware; to guard, inhabit'
wēriġ   adj. 'weary, exhausted'
wearg   adj. 'accursed, wicked'; subst. 'outlaw, criminal' *pl.* wergas
wierġed   adj. 'accursed'
word-hord   'word-resource, vocabulary'
worhte   *p.* 'made, did' *pp.* ġeworht
ġewyrht   FN 'work, deed; desert'
wyrhta   m. 'maker, creator'
wærliċ   = wær adj.
woruld   F. 'world; the contemporary world, life'; tō worulde 'for ever'
woruld–   'worldly, secular-'
wǣrloga   m. 'liar, traitor'
wearm   adj. 'warm'
wyrm   M. 'reptile; dragon'
wyrm-cynn   N. 'reptile, serpent'
warn-að   II 'warns'
-waran   = -ware ('citizens')
wǣron   'were'
weorn-að   II 'fades'
worn/wearn   'large number, crowd, many'
wyrn-eð   'denies, forbids'
weorp-eð/wyrpð   'throws, casts' *pp.* worpen
wyrs   'worse'; wyrst 'worst'
wyrt   F. 'herb, plant'
wyrtrum(a)   Mm. 'root'
wyrtwal-að   II 'uproots'

waroð/wearoð   N. 'shore, beach'
wearð   *p.* 'became'
weorð   adj. 'valuable'; subst. 'value, worth'
weorð-að   'honours, worships' *p.* wurðede
wyrð/weorðeð   'becomes, is (+*pp.*)'
for-weorðeð   'perishes'
weorðmynd   'honour, distinction'

WR*
wracu   F. 'revenge, punishment' *gen.* wræċe
wræcca   m. 'exile, outcast'
wreċeð/wriċð   'drives, expels, utters' *p.* wræċ, wrǣcon *pp.* ġewreċen
wrîdende   'growing, thriving'
ġewrēġed   *pp.* 'agitated'
wrig-að   'advances, twists'
wrugon   'covered' *pp.* ġewriġen
wrāh   *p.* 'covered'
wrîh-ð   'he covers' *pp.* wriġen
wrōht   F. 'accusation, dispute'
wrohton   *ppl.* 'wrought, made'
wrēon   'to cover'
wrenċ   M. 'trick'
wrǣst   adj. 'capable, excellent'
ġewrit   N. 'writing; a writ, a book'
wrît-eð   'he writes' *p.* wrāt
wrǣtliċ   adj. 'ornamental, unusual'
wrîtere   M. 'writer, scribe'
wreð-að   'supports, upholds' *pp.* wreþyd
wrîð-eð   'twists, wraps, binds'
wrāð   adj. 'angry'; subst. 'foe'
wraðe   adv. 'angrily'
wraðu   F. 'support'
ġewrixl   N. '(ex)change, alternation'
wrixl-eð   'exchanges'

61

W*S

wæs	*p.* 'was'
wēas	'by chance'
wîs	adj. 'wise'
wîsa	m. 'leader'
wîse	f. 'way, fashion, manner'
wîs-að	'directs, guides' *p.* wîsode
wıs-að	'demonstrates' *p.* wisode *pp.* ġewissod
ġewiss	adj. 'certain, dependable'
wōs	N. 'juice'
wasc-eð	'washes'
wîsdom	M. 'wisdom'
ġewisslîċe	adv. 'certainly'
wesan	'to be'
wissung	F. 'instruction, guidance'
wâst	'you know'
wēst-eð	'lays waste'
wist	F. 'food; existence'
wiste	*p.* 'he knew'
west	adv. 'west(wards)'
wistlung	F. 'whistling'
wæstm	M. 'growth'; *pl.* wæstmas 'crops, fruits; condition'
wēsten	'wasteland, wilderness'
westan	'from the west'
wēstende	'devastating'
westerne	'westerly'
West-seaxe	*pl.* 'the West Saxons; Wessex'

W*T

wāt	'he knows' *pl.* witon
wæt	adj. 'wet'
wæta	m. 'moisture'
wæt-eð	'wets' *p.* wætte
wîte	N. 'punishment, penalty'
wît-eð	'blames, punishes'
wît-eð	'departs' *p.* ġewāt *pp.* ġewiten
wit	'we two'
wit-an	'to know'

For 16 page catalogue of books on
Anglo-Saxon and related topics, please
send A5 s.a.e. (or second class stamp) to:

Heart of Albion Press
2 Cross Hill Close, Wymeswold,
Loughborough, LE12 6UJ